AIRBORNE

JONATHAN ROTONDO

AIRBORNE

Finding Foxtrot Alpha Mike

GOOSE LANE

Edited by Jill Ainsley.
Cover and page design by Julie Scriver.
Cover images: "Landcape near Tottenham, Ontario" courtesy of Charlie Miller, "*Delta Sierra Alpha* in flight" courtesy of Ernie Szelepcsenyi, "Tony Rotondo with *Foxtrot Alpha Mike*" courtesy of Anna Gaudio.
Text illustrations from the collection of the author, unless otherwise noted.
Printed in Canada.
10 9 8 7 6 5 4 3 2 1

Library and Archives Canada Cataloguing in Publication

Rotondo, Jonathan, 1983-, author
Airborne : finding Foxtrot Alpha Mike / Jonathan Rotondo.
Issued in print and electronic formats.
ISBN 978-1-77310-063-0 (softcover).--ISBN 978-1-77310-064-7 (EPUB).--
ISBN 978-1-77310-065-4 (Kindle)
1. Rotondo, Jonathan, 1983-. 2. Air pilots--Canada--Biography.
3. Fathers and sons--Canada--Biography. 4. Aeronautics.
5. Autobiographies. I. Title.

TL540.R68A3 2019   629.13092   C2018-904641-4
                                        C2018-904642-2

Goose Lane Editions acknowledges the generous financial support of the Government of Canada, the Canada Council for the Arts, and the Province of New Brunswick.

Goose Lane Editions
500 Beaverbrook Court, Suite 330
Fredericton, New Brunswick
CANADA E3B 5X4
www.gooselane.com

To my children, Elgin Anthony and Evelyn Anne,
so that you may know your grandfather and perhaps
understand me a little better than I understood him.

Love,
Dad

Contents

Prologue

I've waited all summer for a day like this: a warm August afternoon cooled by a brisk breeze, bringing lines of neatly formed cumulus clouds marching across the royal blue skies.

The clouds, alike and yet each one unique, advance roughly southeastward. As I roll my biplane out of the shade of the hangar at Rockcliffe Airport in Ottawa, the vanguard of the formation, a loose gaggle of ragged patches, has only just drifted over the field. Ten minutes later, behind the eager tug of the Lycoming engine, we are threading our way northwest through the tip of the main cloud column and climbing quickly.

We stop the climb at our usual seventeen hundred feet and, from our new vantage point inside a cloudless trough, spy a long, solid cloud front stretching across the horizon before us. This new front is the origin of the ragged lines of cumulus clouds that we picked our way through only moments ago. It appears as though a massive, snow-covered mountain has been turned onto its peak so that its low, rolling foothills loom over us like a giant shelf at great altitude. From there, my goggled eyes trace the flanks of the colossus down to a point far in the distance where it vanishes behind the green mounds of the Gatineau Hills.

My mind, when I fly, is quiet. Normally, it's a chaotic mess — though my exterior rarely betrays it. I wasn't always like this. Years ago that stillness and peace was easier to find, and I could hold onto it longer. It happens to all of us — that noise. It is the echo of all our triumphs and failures, our discoveries and losses. Here, aloft, those voices stay far beneath me.

I used to be a daydreamer. I'm not anymore. Life moves too quickly with work and family and obligations to permit the mind to wander. In an airplane, it's equally frowned upon. Flying, after all, is serious business. Still, we're alone up here — the biplane and me. No co-pilot looks at me sideways; I've no passenger to fret over. It's such a lovely afternoon that it would sinful to waste this opportunity for silence and peace.

It was a perfect day for flying. (Photograph courtesy of Bojan Arambasic)

Once again, small groups of white cumulus, having detached themselves from the main body of the cloud front, begin to influence our path, forcing us to circumvent them to the east or west. As one presents itself just below the nose to our right, I pressure the control column slightly aft, and we bound over the top and into a slight right turn. And then, the strangest thing happens. Nature conspires to assemble the perfect set of circumstances — a cloud below, the sun high above and behind us — so that we see our shadow for the first time.

Initially, I wonder what it is, that dark smudge on the cloud's crest ringed in concentric halos of orange, yellow, red, pink, green, and blue. As my eyes blink behind my goggles, I bring the vision into focus. There we are — albeit much larger — complete with twin wings, rounded tail, and the circular shade of the whirling propeller. My other senses dulled, I gaze upon our shadow with the same wonder as one who is seeing their reflection for the first time. With the cloud sliding away, I instinctively bank the wings and roll into a turn to prolong the apparition, but that unwittingly upsets the balance. The image fades.

We fly on. The solid wave of cloud remains distant ahead. The seaplane base at Chelsea, Quebec, drifts by. A trio of float planes, gaily coloured in yellow, orange, and eggshell blue, bob contently at the dock. A canoe works its way south, leaving a feathery wake on the otherwise placid river. Up here, the wind seems stronger, hastening the journey of the clouds drifting our way while hampering our progress up the river.

The cloud bank creeps closer now. It's time. The conditions are ripe for a little cloud-hunting. I raise the nose and inch the throttle forward, adding power to begin a climb. The advantage, after all, is in height. The plane eagerly soars up toward the promise of cooler air. A quick glance at her instruments: the speed stands at ninety miles per hour, the vertical speed announces itself at an optimistic two thousand feet per minute, engine gauges normal, fuel on and sufficient, and switches in their proper places. We are ready.

I push the throttle forward to the stop and pull the plane into a climbing left-hand turn. It bleeds energy quickly: we drift sideways over the top, wings banked vertically, and slide earthward again. With the sun at our back, our first target swims into view between the cabane struts. I feel tension rising in the plane as speed and energy return. I draw a deep breath and depress the trigger on the stick.

The quick burst is ineffectual. Too far away. We close rapidly, the target quivering behind the grey wisp of the racing propeller. The edges of my vision draw away. It is just us and this hapless little cloud.

Another burst. Whitish-grey threads are pulled away and spin off into oblivion. Right stick, right rudder — just the deftest adjustment and the target flashes past our left shoulder. We claw for altitude again as I turn my head this way and that, searching for the next foe.

We roll out of the turn with the nose pointed between twin clouds at a third just above and beyond. The plane roars approval as we descend in a shallow dive toward the first two. This pass must be executed with surgical precision — there will not be another chance.

A stab of left rudder, a brief pause … steady. The plane trembles as we unleash a short burst. Now, before the opportunity has passed, a boot to the right rudder pedal and a longer burst at his companion. The torn cloud rolls away.

I ease the plane's nose up and aim for the leader. My gloved finger depresses the trigger.

Clack. Clack. Clack.

We've played at dogfighting with clouds too long. So long, in fact that either my imagination is entirely devoid of shells or my fantasy Vickers machine gun has jammed. I use the extra speed to rise gently above our would-be target and waggle the wings in salute.

The timbre of the Lycoming's growl changes, tearing the reverie apart. The throttle is a little loose and tends to creep forward. As a result, the engine has picked up about 100 rpm. It's more an idiosyncrasy than an issue, and given that I too have my quirks, I don't see a real need for it to be "fixed." To do so would strip some of this little biplane's personality.

The cloud bank we've been chasing now stretches as far as I can see. As it crawls toward us, I draw in a deep breath. The air up here, measured more or less precisely by our altimeter as 2,750 feet, is violently pure. It nearly burns as you bring it in, and if you hold it for any length of time, it rushes to your head and sets off an electric tingle that crackles and buzzes up and down your spine to your fingers, toes, the tips of your hair.

The cloud bank has grown closer, darker, and more menacing. Somewhere near Wakefield, Quebec, we turn east and follow its billowing edge for a few miles. Every so often, we dip a wing so as to tentatively peek behind the curtain, curious to see what lies beyond. What are we looking for? Something to pursue? A reason to enter a crevasse or fjord carved into this mighty face? Or are we simply searching for inspiration to return home?

We turn west, placing the approaching cloud front on our opposite shoulder. The high flanks of the front have now choked out the sun, dropping the temperature a few degrees. While my biplane seems content to stay aloft and fuel is plentiful, I bank the wings and pick up the river that will lead us home. A feeling of familiarity washes over me. I've flown these skies for a long time. This is home. Soon, the airfield at Rockcliffe will greet me as an old friend.

I give the rudder pedals a playful kick. It's an old custom of mine, something of a nervous tic. The nose wags eagerly in response. In jockeying the pedals, I'm reminding my feet of their true purpose in the impending landing. As graceful a flier and as cute an airplane as she may be, this biplane makes her displeasure known when returning to earth. I approach every landing expecting a kick in the ass.

Before long, the old air force base at Rockcliffe is beyond the plane's long nose. This was my dad's vantage point for all his flights. This is where he once was, where I am now, and where, perhaps, at the intersection of the two, we may meet again. There must be such a place: a field just beyond the horizon where the skies are always blue and the wind is always gentle, where fuel tanks never run dry and hot coffee is never in short supply. At the end of this field, I'll find the spirit of a westward-gone aviator and the spectre of his sprightly mount.

A squeak, a shimmy, and I'm prodded back to reality by the trundling of rubber on runway. Given that her short length predisposes her to swapping ends, my feet work furiously to keep the biplane rolling straight ahead. As we taxi off the runway, we make two left turns and

ASCENT

One

It happens to every pilot: the realization you'd rather be up there than down here. Some can't quite put their finger on the precise moment; they just always knew they'd be happier looking down at the clouds than gazing up at them. Others, like myself, can narrow it down to the exact second. It's our creation moment.

I remember my hair tousled by a breeze that smelled of wet leaves and freshly cut grass. I remember my tiny, pudgy hands closed around a control column. There were rudder pedals, too, but I had no hope of reaching them with my short legs. Beyond, endless feather tails of wispy clouds drifted on a sea of brilliant blue, their ends curling like so many serene smiles. The airplane rocked and sighed in the wind. I felt safe and comfortable.

Then, two strong hands grabbed me under my arms and lifted me high above a little red-and-white biplane. I floated above it for a moment, looking down at the top wing and fuselage. They had been dirty when my dad sat me down an hour before. Now, her rosy skin gleamed in the late afternoon sunshine. My feet hit the ground. As my dad led me away, I turned to look at the airplane. The arrangement of the air intakes made it seem as though the little biplane was smiling at me. I waved and giggled.

It was the late spring of 1988. I was four years old and I was saying goodbye to the Smith Miniplane known by the call sign *Charlie Foxtrot Foxtrot Alpha Mike* — or *FAM* for short. It would be twenty-five years before I'd ever sit in a Smith again, and two more before I would find myself at the controls of one in flight.

My dad logged relatively few hours in his Miniplane — barely fifty — but the effect those precious hours and minutes had on him was immeasurable. He had time in dozens of airplanes doing everything from aerobatics to instrument flying, but in the sanctum of *Foxtrot Alpha Mike*'s single seat, he discovered the true meaning of the miracle of flight. *FAM* had the rare ability to slow and even stop time. On twin crimson wings soaring above the patchwork farmers' fields of Ontario, my father escaped the temporal bonds of earthly woes — at least until fuel level became a concern. Even on the ground, *FAM* seemed hell-bent on flight. Squatting on her landing gear, nose pointed stubbornly aloft, wings and flying wires braced like muscle and sinew, she seemed to say, "Hey, that's where we ought to be, so what are we waiting for?"

There are two kinds of pilot. The first group regards their machines as living, breathing aerial companions that understand and empathize, reward and punish, give and take life — but always poetically, heroically, rich in grace and with a certain measure of mechanical humanity. The second group sees them as machines to fly, and that's it. My dad and I were of the former persuasion. We, some would say unwisely, applied human characteristics to mere machines. The latter group may understand but privately regards us as batty.

So when my dad sold his Smith in 1988, he lost a companion. As I grew up, we spoke constantly of flying, and after I gained my license, we flew together. Even as our relationship changed, grew difficult as the years wore on and sickness taxed his body and mind, flying *FAM* remained a ready topic. My dad would tell brilliant stories and paint vivid pictures of what it was like cocooned in her open cockpit. I felt as though I had truly come along on all their fantastic adventures. He talked about that airplane like an old girlfriend who had broken his heart. Every time I suggested tracking the plane down, he'd brush it off. There'd be a tightness in his voice, as he'd say he had no interest in knowing where the plane was or what it was doing or who had the fortune of flying it. He cared only for where it had been, what it had been like to fly it, and how it made him feel.

⊙

The type of airplane that made such an impact on my father began its life in a garage in California in the 1950s. I picture a slight man, a stick of chalk in his fingers as he crouches on the floor, drawing the outline of a plane's snub-nosed cowling. The chalk grinds as it passes over the rough concrete. Frank Smith frowns and rubs away a wayward line with his palm before resuming his work. The flat light of a southern California evening is leaking into the shade of the garage, casting long shadows on the floor. Chalk dust rises slowly from the concrete to mingle with the fine sand thrown up by the breeze. He rises, takes a few steps back, and, tucking the chalk into his shirt pocket, places his hands on his hips, admiring his creation. He nods in satisfaction.

As a boy, Frank Smith built model airplanes and gliders, but it was a flight in a Curtiss-Wright Junior out of a barnstormer's field in Missouri that convinced him that flying was for him. The Depression shelved his dreams of flight for more than a decade. During the war, now living in California and working as a machinist, Smith returned to building models and the gasoline engines that powered them, if only as a way to break up his long working hours. In 1949, Smith finally earned his pilot's license and bought an old Travel Air biplane that had seen better days. Using the skills acquired over many years of model-making, he restored the Travel Air and began building his flight experience. The Travel Air, however, was big and sluggish and didn't fit Smith's idea of what an airplane should be.

In the early fifties, Smith met another early home builder, Ray Stits, who had recently completed a homebuilt aircraft of his own design, which he dubbed the Playboy. Smith taught himself to weld and built a Playboy of his own. (A modified Playboy was also the first home-built aircraft ever built and registered in Canada; Keith S. Hopkinson's example is part of the Canada Aviation and Space Museum collection.)

Smith, however, was still not satisfied. In his mind, the Playboy still lacked something. Knowing he was partial to biplanes, Smith's friends suggested he add another wing to Stits's design. Smith, both a dreamer and a doer, had other ideas, and one evening he picked up that piece of chalk.

Unlike many dreamers, Smith didn't stop with a chalk outline on his garage floor. Something about the idea gnawed at him, spurred him on. The plane had to be designed with the weekend hobby pilot in mind — simple and straightforward so that an average craftsman with readily available tools could scrounge materials and build it in a reasonable amount of time. And so, from the chalk outline rose a short fuselage with a delicately rounded tail sitting on a simple set of conventional landing gear. Twin wings of wood, only seventeen feet long, sprouted from its body of metal tubing, and were joined together by the struts and wires characteristic of biplanes since the dawn of flight. Inside the close confines of the single cockpit, Smith fitted basic flight and engine controls along with the few necessary instruments. A 100 horsepower engine was hung on the front and enveloped in a cowling of sheet metal. The rest of the machine was covered in fabric that was treated and then heated to shrink taut around the biplane's form. Smith painted his biplane in a coat of '56 Ford yellow, with accents in WACO red and a black cheatline from nose to tail. He christened his creation the DSA-1 Miniplane — for "damned small airplane."

Smith first flew his biplane on October 29, 1956, only eight months after his chalk sketch. His creation wasn't fast or powerful. It wouldn't win any air races or impress crowds with death-defying aerial stunts. And yet it was so much *fun*. It took all the sweetest, most beautiful aspects of flight — the freedom, the rush of the wind, the lightness in your heart — and brought them together. In this way, the Smith is greater than the sum of its parts and, in that sense, it is perfect.

The following year, Smith's friend Lee Wainscott drew up the plans and the joyful little biplane was offered to anyone with enough time, effort, love, and patience to build a dream. That rudimentary outline on the floor of Smith's garage became one of the most popular homebuilt aircraft ever to take flight. It was so eagerly accepted that a period magazine called it "America's Biplane Sweetheart." The Smith is

The very first Smith Miniplane, the prototype registered N90P,
in flight over California in the late fifties.

(Photograph courtesy of Dorothy Smith)

a throwback to leather flying caps, gauntlets, pencil-thin moustaches, and twinkling eyes behind oil-speckled goggles. It belongs in a world of sun-swept grass fields, open cockpits, and boot-scuffed floorboards, where the air smells of oil and gasoline and "Contact!" is bellowed before a propeller whirls around and an engine purrs. Simply put, the Smith is every pilot's dream — a vehicle in which they can taste the pure, basic, unadulterated fun of flight.

Smith, however, never saw the popularity of his design, having died of a heart attack in 1958, when he was only forty-two. His death was felt deeply; Smith had lent his time and expertise to many early home builders embarking on their own projects. At the time of his death, fifteen Miniplanes were in construction. By the early 1970s, three hundred and fifty sets of plans had been sold, and more than two hundred examples were flying in the United States and Canada. Everyone who ever climbed into a Miniplane and opened the throttle continued Frank Smith's work, including my father, Antonio Rotondo, and, much later, me.

Every single Miniplane is unique, even if you can't tell them apart by sight — a custom-built reflection of the builder's particular set of preferences and the embodiment of a dream. In those days, there were no kits of pre-fabricated parts. These were handmade, flying works of art, carved out of wood and forged from metal in the same way a fine musical instrument is created. The craftsmen who built these machines were a unique breed. As their ranks thinned over time, their airplanes flew less often, and the market to sell them softened. With each unfulfilled opportunity, time dulled their skills and rust began to spot their confidence. Reluctance turned into trepidation and then to fear. Occasionally, the little biplanes would change hands and the new owners, long on excitement but short on common sense, would scare themselves half to death on the first landing and then content themselves with telling war stories. Slowly, most Miniplanes faded from record — either abandoned in the back of a hangar, cracked up in an accident and forgotten, or left outside to rot in the sun. An estimated twenty-five Miniplanes were built in Canada. *Foxtrot Alpha Mike* was one of the last survivors. Now, there are only two or three still flying in Canada and not many more in the United States.

Flying is magical. Of course, it's far more technical than that. I can explain how a curved surface passing through the air generates lift and how you can simulate the same by sticking your hand out of a moving car's window: Bernoulli's principle, fluid dynamics, differences in pressure, and all that. In the end, they're only words and equations that fall hopelessly short of describing what people living barely two hundred years ago might have described as sorcery.

All of this started in 1903 with the Wright brothers and a flight of just 102 feet above some sand dunes in Kitty Hawk, North Carolina. With Orville at the controls, the Wright Flyer remained barely airborne for twelve seconds. Almost sixty-six years later, Neil Armstrong set foot on the surface of the moon, carrying with him a piece of wood from the Wright Flyer's left propeller and a swatch of fabric from its wing.

What would the world look like if, in the early days of flight, when most experiments ended in crashes, the pioneers and dreamers simply gave up? Jean-François Pilâtre de Rozier and Pierre Romain misjudged their vaulting of the English Channel in a balloon in the late eighteenth century and became the first fatalities of an air crash. In 1908, Thomas Selfridge smashed his skull in Virginia on a flight piloted by Oliver Wright, and in 1911, Édouard Bague vanished into thin air somewhere over the Mediterranean. Their ghosts were only the first. Whether by waxwing, balloon, dirigible, or airplane, history is littered with the bodies of pioneer aviators who launched into the unknown and paid the ultimate price.

But we pressed on. For every failure were multiple successes. Louis Blériot made the first flight across the English Channel in 1909. Soon after the guns of the Great War fell silent, a United States Navy crew hopscotched their way across the Atlantic Ocean in a flying boat, followed barely a month later by Britons John Alcock and Arthur Brown, who made the trip without stopping. Within a decade, Charles Lindbergh became the first man and then Amelia Earhart the first woman to accomplish the feat, non-stop and on their own. Soon, vaulting oceans gave way to circling the globe. Distance, altitude, and speed records were set and broken almost daily. Planes shuttled first the mail and then paying passengers across countries and around the globe. The airplane quickly eclipsed trains and ships as the preferred way to travel and, along the way, shrank the world.

☺

My father's death hit me harder than anything else I'd faced in my life, before or since. After years of distance and difficulty, we had just started to build a new relationship. I was twenty-eight years old, on the cusp of starting my own family, and while his passing was by no means unexpected, I was not ready to say goodbye. Everything that followed happened so quickly and with such severity that I could do nothing but flip a switch and function purely on autopilot. A few months after my father died, after the frenetic pace of the wake, funeral, and burial had eased, and people stopped visiting or asking me how I was doing, I only felt cold and numb. I hadn't mourned my father — not yet, at least — and now I was well beyond tears. My grief hardened. I began to feel guilty and angry. I felt I had failed my father in some way, and I needed something productive and meaningful to occupy me.

Increasingly, my thoughts turned to Dad's biplane, and I decided to track her down. So began years of work in aircraft archeology, self-reflection, and discovery. Using the phone book, internet searches, and some old-fashioned detective skills picked up during my years as a journalist, I pieced together the biplane's story after we lost track of her. I worked backwards, too: pushing through cobwebbed memories to discover both the airplane's and my dad's histories before they came together. The journey has been both uplifting and crushing, often in the same moment. A guilt that will forever haunt me has spurred me on. But I needed to find a way to preserve my father and the airplane he loved so dearly — to give them both a measure of immortality.

Two

At around the time Frank Smith was using a wood file and a welding torch to turn his dream into a reality, my dad was tending sheep in the fields of San Giacomo degli Schiavoni, a small village near the Adriatic coastal town of Termoli, about where the base of the calf begins on the Italian boot. San Giacomo is in the province of Campobasso, which is part of the region of Molise, a charming region of craggy hills, sunflower-choked fields, pristine sandy beaches, and sapphire-blue waters. In the fall of 1945 roughly twelve hundred people called it home. The town's population hasn't varied by more than a dozen since then.

My father's parents were Giovanni and Donata (née Sorgini) Rotondo. They were tenant farmers, growing wheat and corn on rented land, and had originally moved to the area from a village in the neighbouring province to the north. My grandmother had a fifth-grade education, which was advanced for the time. My grandfather had gone as far as the third grade. When the Second World War broke out, he was conscripted into the Italian Army as a private and sent to Italian-occupied Libya.

My father's origin was linked to a peculiar moonless night near Tripoli in January 1943. My grandfather and a fellow soldier were on sentry duty, huddled together in a foxhole dug into the gritty desert sand. It was cold. They couldn't smoke because the glow from their cigarettes would give away their position to the British soldiers lurking in the gloom. The war was going badly for the Italians. They had invaded Egypt, been pushed out, counterattacked, and failed again. They would have been driven into the sea if it wasn't for German

(l to r) Uncle Dante and Dad,
in Termoli, Italy, 1954.

support that helped them hold on to Libya for a time. Now, their days were numbered. Somewhere in the inky darkness before them stood the British Eighth Army. Behind them, they could almost hear the Mediterranean Sea lapping at the shore.

Around two in the morning, they heard a sound: a thud followed by scraping, as though someone had stumbled and fallen into the sand. My grandfather and his mate snapped to attention and pointed their rifles toward the sound, staring down the long barrels into the nothingness. My grandfather called out the challenge phrase, and they listened for the correct reply. They got it but the voice was breathless and raspy, and as they lowered their guns, they were surprised to see their battalion deputy commander, a major, scramble past them into the camp.

The next morning, both soldiers were called into the major's tent and asked if they would like to go home for some rest and recuperation. They accepted and were put on an airplane by lunchtime. While they were returning home to their families the next day, their entire battalion surrendered to the British. The major had crossed the line to negotiate terms of surrender and, having been intercepted on his return by my grandfather and his friend, was concerned the plan would be foiled, so he sent them away. Otherwise, my grandfather would have been captured with the rest of his unit.

Antonio Francesco Rotondo came into the world in 1945. Some confusion surrounds the exact time of my father's birth. My grandmother maintained (and she should know) that he was born on September 2, after midnight. When anyone pointed out the obvious — after midnight is the third — she would just scoff. At any rate, the stone walls of the house he was born in still stand. The roof has long since rotted away, however, and the ever-present sunflowers that grow like weeds now call it home.

Thirteen people lived in the house: Dad's parents, his paternal grandparents, two aunts, two uncles, and, eventually, five children. The nearest elementary school was five miles away, and my dad walked there and back for his entire first year. In the second grade, he lived with his maternal grandparents in the village where his parents were born. His grandparents didn't treat him well, however, and Dad found living away from his family difficult.

He liked hunting. He once built a makeshift pistol that promptly backfired and put a rather large hole in his cheek that left a scar. He was an atrocious athlete and won the dubious nickname *mani de merda* — literally "hands of shit." An inattentive shepherd prone to losing his charges, he found his books more absorbing than his duties and would spend his days studying in the shade of a tree. Only the faraway hum of a passing airplane at altitude would tear him from his studies. Looking up, he wondered what flight would feel like and thought that, some day, he might be an aviator too.

The first airplane he saw up close was hardly recognizable as such. It was the wreck of a twin-engined British Royal Air Force bomber that had been shot down on a raid during the war. It had come down on a plateau atop a gently sloping hill near my father's village. Some of the crew had managed to parachute to safety, but at least three, including the pilot in the cockpit, died. By the time my dad was old enough to poke around the site, very little of the airplane remained: bits of fuselage, a landing gear leg, half of the tattered tail creaking in the wind. My dad remembered that plants refused to take root in the scarred earth, and sifting through the dirt with your fingers would bring up coins, buttons emblazoned with a crowned eagle, and, one time, a tin comb with melted teeth.

These relics were left where they were found partly out of respect, but mostly out of superstition and fear. An aunt, who many in the village believed could "see things," warned that the pilot's ghost had sat atop the airplane's burned-out fuselage in the days and weeks following the crash. And while much of the wreck had long since been removed, she believed his spirit kept watch over his former mount.

My dad had a younger brother, Dante, and three younger cousins who were like siblings. My father was a serious kid. The face gazing out from old photographs is almost expressionless: mouth turned down at the ends but not frowning, eyes dark and pensive, ears that stick out perhaps a bit more than you'd like. In group shots, while the other kids are smiling or halfway through a laugh, my dad remains stoic, focussed. He parted his dark hair on the left, and a few strands of hair were prone to fall across his brow. He was of slender build, and while he wasn't by any means tall (he was five foot six as an adult), his longish arms and spindly legs might have given you that impression.

Dad returned home for high school. He loved learning, did well at school, and figured that education would be his ticket to something greater somewhere else. When many of his peers walked away from their education after finishing high school, my dad wanted to go to college. My grandparents knew my dad was bright, and they scraped together enough money for tuition, books, and clothes. A few years later, he graduated from a local college with the title of geometrist — a sort of hybrid draftsman and civil engineer. He was hired soon after to work as a land surveyor but he despised it; he found the work boring and felt he was destined for something greater. My grandmother reminded him of the sacrifices she had made. The financial burden of putting my dad through school had been significant. If the work was not to his liking, she suggested, then perhaps he should look abroad. He had an aunt and a cousin living in Toronto. He could start there. Soon after, at not quite twenty, fuelled by the promise of adventure and a desire to leave home and with an airplane ticket purchased by my grandfather, he left for a job in Canada. The ten-hour flight out of Rome was his first time in an airplane.

He lived with his aunt and cousin in Toronto and began working a survey gig on municipal and provincial roadwork projects. It was hard, dirty work that wasn't particularly challenging. Apart from the boredom, the road survey crews were regularly subjected to painful asphalt and tar burns. While moving some piping out of his way, my dad developed a hernia, which required surgery. It took two months for him to recover. He spent the time learning English.

Once he'd healed from the surgery, my dad took up judo, but his life was largely limited to work. For the first time in his life, he had the money to buy nice things. Canada was a whole new world: young and modern. Gone were the dirt roads and rolling hills of his childhood. Everyone seemed to have a gleaming new car. They had style. Dad began to identify as a Canadian. He had more love for his adoptive country than the one of his birth. Italy had held him back. Canada helped him realize his dreams.

When my uncle graduated from high school in 1967, Dad convinced him to come to Canada. But only a few months after Uncle Dante arrived, my dad left. A Swiss company was looking for people to work on infrastructure projects in Vietnam and East Africa. Given the escalating war in Vietnam, my dad opted for Africa and, at age twenty-three, he found himself as project manager, charged with building a water treatment plant in Bukoba, Tanzania.

My father was the only white man in the crew. And while some of his colleagues knew a little English or Italian, my dad learned and insisted on working in Swahili. His easy smile, almost obsessive dedication to learning the language, and willingness to work shoulder to shoulder with the men in the trenches of the job site endeared him to the locals. He wouldn't hesitate to coax a temperamental generator to life or jump into knee-deep mud to help make a last-second adjustment before the concrete was poured. If the job was done well, he was generous with his praise, and if not, it would be done again — correctly this time — after a humbling and educational talk. He developed the reputation of being tough but fair, and quickly "Mister Tony" became simply "Tony."

Still, despite success on the job site, life in East Africa was tough. At first, my dad lived in the captain's cabin of a rustbucket freighter moored to the shore of Lake Victoria. There was little to do except work, sweat, burn in the sun, fend off the mosquitos, and worry about malaria.

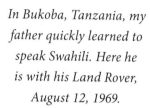

In Bukoba, Tanzania, my father quickly learned to speak Swahili. Here he is with his Land Rover, August 12, 1969.

My dad wasn't one for vices; in fact, he hardly drank. He enjoyed wine because it was always on the table as he was growing up, but he deplored anything in excess. In his mind, getting blind drunk even a few times was the mark of an alcoholic. Despite this, he was once arrested, along with his entire crew of workers, for threatening a bar owner who refused to serve them. They had just spent eighteen hours pouring concrete and needed to put out some fires, but the bar was closed. A few heatstroke- and fatigue-fuelled words later, and the local police were called. And on another sticky night, he came home with a paper bag filled with basement gin and vermouth and proceeded to drink it all. When he shot a fern, his only living household companion, full of holes with a pellet gun because he had nothing better to do, he figured he needed a hobby. He didn't have to wait long.

After two years in Bukoba, the company transferred him to a water treatment plant project in Nairobi. They set him up in his own house with a gardener, a cook, and a housekeeper. The Kenyan capital, a five-hour flight from Bukoba, was a much larger, more vibrant city — and it had an airport that hosted not one but two flying schools. In July 1970 my dad walked through the doors of Wilken Aviation at the Wilson Airport on the southern outskirts of Nairobi, and asked about learning to fly.

The wonder and excitement of launching into the sky for the first time is one of those life-altering moments that burns into your soul. For my dad, that day came on July 15, 1970.

The mechanics of flying are not difficult. A control stick rising from the floor or a wheel protruding from the panel allows the pilot to raise and lower the nose or turn the airplane left or right. Pedals on the floor allow the pilot to drive — or taxi — the airplane on the ground, and in the air the same controls move a rudder, which swings the nose left or right. A throttle lever, worked by hand, functions in the same way as an accelerator in a car. An instrument panel supplies the pilot with the necessary information: airspeed, altitude, engine oil temperature and pressure, fuel quantity, and so on. The pilot must learn to interpret this information and use it to inform the manipulation of the controls and thereby guide their ship through the sky.

My dad was twenty-four years old when he took the pilot's seat for the first time, in a Piper PA-28-140 Cherokee only recently delivered from the factory in faraway Vero Beach, Florida. Wilken Aviation ran a thriving flight school and charter business out of Nairobi's Wilson Airport. The outfit, staffed by ex-pat Britons, Australians, and a handful of Canadians, was also the African dealer for Piper Aircraft. Students not only learned to fly but did so on nearly new machines that had not yet suffered the tortures of flight training. In the right seat was rookie instructor pilot Murray Sinton, an Australian. My father was his first student. More than forty years later, my dad remembered him fondly as his best instructor.

It was a work day, and Dad was likely on his lunch break. At any rate, he was the boss, and who would question him if he stole away for an hour? Furthermore, who would find him in the skies above Nairobi? My dad was excited. The Directorate of Civil Aviation of the East African Community had only just issued him his student pilot license the day before this first flight. The weather in Nairobi was typical for the season: sunny with a few puffs of cumulus and a pleasant 21°C. Despite the moderate climate, it was stuffy inside the Cherokee's cockpit, so Sinton propped the only door open with his foot, and the tiny storm window on my dad's side of the canopy hung open. A soft breeze drifted back from the slowly turning propeller.

Piper Cherokee 5Y-ALG breaks formation near Nairobi on March 25, 1971. Chief pilot Alan Coulson appears to be riding right seat. My dad sent this photo to his youngest cousin and noted on the back that these airplanes could reach speeds of 150 miles per hour with four people on board — a slight exaggeration. This aircraft suffered an unspecified accident at Savani Airstrip near Nandi, Kenya, in November 1974.

After receiving clearance from the tower, Sinton yanked the door closed and snapped the lock above his head. He called for my dad to close the storm window before advancing the throttle. The Cherokee, the registration *5Y-AJJ* painted on each side of the fuselage, then began rolling forward — engine at full power, Sinton's left hand on the throttle and his right resting on the control yoke. Wilson Airport sits at just over a mile above sea level, so Sinton held the boxy trainer on the runway a few beats longer than usual before easing the yoke back. The Cherokee's wheels left the ground, and my father was hooked forever.

The flight lasted only half an hour. The notations in my dad's logbook, set down in his hand almost fifty years ago, betray none of the emotions he felt that day. On cream-coloured paper in blue ink, the particulars of the flight are recorded dispassionately: date, aircraft type, registration, captain, duration, etc. In the remarks section of his then-new logbook, he wrote only "No. 3," the lesson number for "Effects of Flight Controls."

My dad continued his training under Sinton's careful tutelage almost daily. They got along well. Together, they progressed from the basics of straight and level flight, climbs, descents, and turns to stalls and spins. As my father's skill and confidence grew, Sinton introduced more complex concepts and more difficult exercises. They spent a fair amount of time — thirteen hours over fifteen lessons — working on landing. That's the rub about learning to fly: taking off is the easy part; all the skill and finesse go into safely returning the aircraft to earth with a reasonable expectation of being able to use it again.

On his twenty-fifth birthday, my dad woke at the ungodly hour of four in the morning and drove his Land Rover to Wilson Airport. The red dust churned up by his tires caught the rising sun in gritty flashes of tawny golds and browns. The air of the September dawn was pleasantly crisp and cool. In the distance, an airplane's engine coughed and caught.

That day's lesson was the circuit, the racetrack pattern around and above an airport's runway that planes join in order to land. The circuit has four parts, or "legs," that can be flown in either a left- or right-hand direction, depending on the procedures in place at the airport. The first leg is known as the departure. The aircraft climbs straight out into the wind and away from the runway. Next, at about five hundred feet above the ground, the aircraft turns onto the crosswind leg and continues the climb to the circuit altitude, which is generally one thousand feet above the ground. The aircraft then turns again to position itself on the downwind leg with the wind at her back and the airport roughly a quarter mile away to the side. The final two legs are known as base, opposite to the crosswind leg and with the aircraft descending, and final, the last segment lining the airplane up to land on the runway. My father had these patterns around each of Wilson's two runways etched in his mind. He could, if he wished (and was devoid of any common sense), fly the circuit with his eyes closed. For exactly one month, all he had been doing was takeoffs and landings, downwind and pre-landing checks, rotations and round-outs. For most of that time, Murray Sinton sat next to him. That day was different. When my father yelled "Clear!" and cranked the engine, the instructor was Paul Lennox, who was checking Sinton's instruction.

At 6:15 a.m., the plane climbed away from Wilson Airport. The plains were beginning to boil under the African sun. Half an hour and four circuits later, the Cherokee returned to earth and taxied slowly to the Wilken ramp. Lennox shoved the door open against the propeller's idle breath and slid out onto the wing. He turned back, crouched behind the shield of the door, cupped his hand to his mouth, and shouted a few words to my dad. A curt nod, and Lennox pushed the door closed. He clapped his right hand on the top of the Cherokee's cabin and stepped off the wing's trailing edge. He walked backwards for a few feet as the Cherokee's engine picked up and the plane taxied for the runway.

Alpha Juliet India rattled into the air with my dad at the controls —

on his own for the first time. It is every pilot's first test, and every pilot's most private feat of accomplishment. It is a rite of passage that returns you to earth changed, older, with a hint of swagger in your step and a heart swelling with pride.

The environment my dad chose to learn to fly in posed particular challenges. In Africa, depending on the season, entire lakes could vanish, making navigation difficult, and vast swaths of the landscape were barren and inhospitable year-round. Many of the airfields in East Africa were little more than a patch of flat savannah where traffic had reduced the long grass to stubble. Animals often took up residence in these areas, and pilots were advised to fly several low passes before landing in order to clear a path. Nor were the animals the only obstacles. Pieces of elephant dung, the size of small boulders and dense enough to tear off a plane's landing gear, were ignored at the pilot's peril.

My dad earned his wings in May 1971 after passing the private flight test on his first attempt. He had used nine pages of his logbook and logged sixty-two hours and five minutes of flight time, nearly twelve of which were solo. A man named McAuliffe signed him off. All the men who sat next to him — Murray Sinton, Paul Lennox, Mike Amos, Clive Corner, and Alan Coulson — had a hand in shaping my father as a pilot. Sinton, by far, made the greatest impression. My dad also spoke fondly and often of Coulson, the chief pilot. Amos was known to rap his students on the knees with a bony fist if they made a mistake. Either Lennox or Corner carried a penknife, reportedly as a way to swiftly and painfully bring a student back to reality in the event they ever froze on the controls and thus lessened the instructor's chance of an old man's peaceful death.

I'd like to think that the aircraft my father learned on are lovingly tended to and still flying, but they are likely gone. One crashed in 1973 after running out of fuel on a cross-country flight, killing the pilot and lone occupant. Two others were involved in accidents in Kenya in the 1970s. The fourth crashed into the Rufiji River in

Tanzania in 1985. The plane was destroyed, but the pilot survived. Of the others, perhaps some are rotting in the African sun, pushed up behind a Quonset hangar in the corner of an overgrown field. Their once-shiny aluminum skin is pockmarked and bleeding rivulets of reddish-brown rust. Registrations have worn off; yellowish padding bursts through the cracks in the vinyl seats; windshields are chipped, yellowed, and cobwebbed.

Aviators live, and often die, in spectacular fashion. Three of my dad's friends during his time in Africa stared death in the face — and two blinked. The first flew into power lines while on a pleasure flight with his pregnant wife. While stopping at a remote dirt strip on a solo cross-country trip, another taxied into a small ditch. He likely pulled on the propeller to try to free the aircraft but left the magneto ignition switches on. The engine caught, decapitating him. They found him two days later with the aircraft standing silent guard. Her fuel tanks had run dry.

Despite the risks, my dad took to flying with a voracious appetite. As soon as he finished his private license, he began finding and mastering new airplanes: the venerable Piper Super Cub, the stalwart Chipmunk trainer, and the graceful Fournier RF-5. These experiences would be his first tastes of taildraggers and aerobatics which would, in turn, lead him to his favourite plane, ten years later.

Three

Dad knew that, to become a better pilot, he needed to seek out new experiences and challenges even if they scared him. He also knew that if he wanted to fly the really interesting or high performance machines — classics, vintages, warbirds, aerobatic, or bush planes — he had to learn to fly what's known in aviation as a tailwheel. A tailwheel airplane, as the name implies, features two main wheels under the forward fuselage and a smaller, single wheel located beneath the tail. On the ground, the aircraft sits with her nose pointed aloft and the tail low. In some cases, generally in biplanes or in aircraft with large engines and long noses, the pilot's view straight ahead, at least on the ground, can be limited.

Most pilots train on aircraft with tricycle landing gear: two main wheels and a smaller wheel under the nose. On the ground, the airplane sits in a level stance or even slightly nose low. Cessna dubbed this configuration "Land-O-Matic," implying that the plane can land itself. That's not entirely true, but one can land a tricycle-gear airplane by planting it on the ground at pretty much any angle and, after some squealing from the tires, have it right itself and roll merrily along. This is thanks to the clever engineers who placed the centre of gravity ahead of the main wheels. If the aircraft does not touch down in line with its direction of travel, gravity takes corrective action and pulls the airplane into line again.

Taildraggers, however, have the centre of gravity behind the main wheels, so when the aircraft touches down at an angle, the centre of gravity tries to pull the tail around. If unchecked, this swing can become a ground loop, causing the airplane to veer away from its desired direction of travel or spin in a circle. A ground loop can result in a wingtip dragged along the ground, the failure of the landing gear, or the aircraft cartwheeling and flipping over onto its back. These machines require a firm hand, some measure of attention, and functioning feet. Dad had only to look across the ramp to the Aero Club of East Africa to find just the pilot to teach him how to fly a tailwheel.

James Nigel Hamilton was born near the Red Sea in Hurghada, Egypt, in 1922 as his mother rushed home from Singapore to give birth in England. The baby wouldn't wait, and when he came out with his fists clenched and punching at the air, his family nicknamed him Biff.

As a very young child, Biff watched the birds soar above and hoped that he might one day be so lucky as to fly. As soon as he graduated from high school, Biff joined the Royal Air Force and was sent to South Africa to train as a pilot. Once he'd earned his wings, he returned to England and trained other instructors who would in turn tutor front-line combat pilots. King George VI awarded him the Air Force Cross. "This officer," his citation reads, "has, throughout, set an exceptionally high standard and the results obtained by his flight reflect his outstanding devotion to duty and fine example in the air."

Almost two years after the war's end, Biff left the Royal Air Force and started a garage with two friends from the force. His mates repaired and serviced vehicles while Biff ran a taxi service in an old Rolls Royce. Not long afterwards, he went to work in Nigeria where he managed a banana plantation. He did well, although he joked that his promotions were merely the result of not dying from malaria. Thirteen years and a few job changes later, he came into the possession of a Piper Cub — for decades the embodiment of freedom of flight — and flew it across Africa, establishing flying clubs wherever the wind took him.

It wasn't just former air force pilots who shaped post-war aviation in Africa. When Thornhill, the Royal Air Force's training school in the British colony of Southern Rhodesia, closed in the early fifties, it decided to dispose of the de Havilland DHC-1 Chipmunks that were its primary training aircraft locally. The demobilized Chipmunks were relatively new, readily available, and cheap. Having risen from the drawing board of a Polish engineer in a Toronto plant, the Chipmunk is perhaps one of the nicest airplanes ever designed. Dubbed "the poor man's Spitfire," she's graceful and elegant. The plucky little trainers could be bought for as little as £500. The Kenyan Air Force bought several, and a dozen more found their way into civilian hands. At Wilson Airport near Nairobi, the Aero Club of East Africa bought at least three, possibly six. Biff joined the Aero Club and began teaching aerobatics on the "Chippie" shortly before meeting my dad.

Biff and my dad worked together for five flights, building and honing the coordination skills needed to handle a tailwheel aircraft.

"Left rudder, left rudder, left rudder!" Biff's voice fought the roar of the engine.

Unlike most North American airplanes, the Chipmunk's propeller turns counter-clockwise when viewed from the pilot's seat, and aerodynamic forces collude to push the airplane to the right. The pilot uses the rudder pedals to counteract these forces and keep the aircraft tracking straight, hence Biff's shouted instructions. But Biff's pupil did not react. The airplane, at a comically slow pace, wandered to the right edge of the runway.

"Move your feet!" Biff jockeyed the pedals. The nose waggled left and right in response.

"Stick forward!" Biff called out. The response from the front seat was feeble. "Stick forward!"

"More?" my father called back hesitantly. He strained against his shoulder harness, trying to catch a glimpse of his instructor and, perhaps, a measure of reassurance.

"Don't look at me! Watch where we're going!" Biff hollered in reply. "And yes, more forward stick!"

"Why?" asked my dad. They say there are no stupid questions. They're wrong. The airplane lurched into the air — sideways, naturally — and behind the strength of its 145 horsepower Gipsy Major engine it took off a little earlier than it should.

"That's why." Then: "Fly the damned airplane." Biff's gentle tone softened the bite of his words. "Don't hang onto it as if you're walking the family dog."

Flying was my dad's only real pastime away from his job. He flew almost every day. But flying alone was not enough to keep him happy. Dad hadn't seen his parents or any member of his family other than his brother since he left Italy in 1965. They had only a vague idea of where he was and what he was doing. He wrote to his family in Italy and to his brother in Toronto that he was building an airplane. His letters didn't indicate whether he'd acquired plans and was building his airplane from scratch or if he'd bought a project he hoped to complete. His intention was to fly this airplane home to San Giacomo, almost three thousand miles as the crow flies, and certainly much more if he took a less direct route and avoided long legs over water. It was a fantastical plan bordering on insanity, one I find hard to reconcile with the father I knew, who would hesitate to hang a picture.

The water treatment plant that my dad was charged with building included a system of water tanks located on hills overlooking the city. Rather than shuttle workers to and from the site daily, the company built temporary shelters: small clapboard shacks topped with roofs of woven straw. The workers, including my dad, slept in hammocks or on raised cots. The crews would live on the job site for a few days at a time while working on the tanks and then return to the main project site.

On one humid night in June, my dad was woken up in the middle of the night by the sound of laboured breathing. As the boss, Dad had his own hut, but he was convinced that someone was standing next to him. He had the unshakeable impression that it was his father. The breathing continued as Dad fumbled for a flashlight, but it stopped as soon as the beam clicked on and illuminated the empty hut.

Sensing something was wrong, he dressed quickly, jumped into the Land Rover, and raced into town to the post office box he kept. There he found a telegram sent two days earlier: *Antonio. Father is not well. Come home.*

While my father didn't know it, my grandfather was already dead, having passed away suddenly after a stroke. The telegram had been sent to bring him home under the impression that his father was still alive. That morning, he flew to Rome, and then rented a car to make the lonely, three-hour drive east to his home. When he reached Termoli, the larger town near his village, he saw the death notices for his father and learned the truth.

He spent that summer in Italy and returned to Nairobi in September, still grieving. Not much had changed at Wilson Airport. Biff was still at it. The Chipmunks sat in a neat row, their highly polished aluminum skins shimmering in the sunlight, beckoning. Some had been retired and put up for sale, and my dad seriously considered buying one, but another siren's song soared higher. In my dad's absence, Wilken had acquired a brand-new Sportavia RF-5 — a light sport motor-glider with gorgeous lines. The pilot could take off and fly under the power of the engine but had the option of shutting down the engine and gliding to earth. Over the next few weeks, my dad learned to fly this unique craft and found unlimited promise in its gull-like grace.

Next came aerobatics. Aerobatics is perhaps the purest form of flying: simple, unadulterated, and boundless fun. I abhor the term *stunt flying*; it smacks of haphazardness and chance. In reality, aerobatics is both a science and an art, a calculated and beautiful display of what pilot and machine can accomplish when they become one. The pilot must keep airspeed, energy, and altitude in delicate balance. If you've ever watched an aerobatic display at an air show or taken a ride on an extreme roller coaster, you have some idea. There is, however, no substitute for living the experience — it is nearly impossible to describe in a way that does it justice.

Aerobatics exerts significant forces on the body. In a loop, for example, where the aircraft carves a vertical circle, the pilot typically withstands 4 Gs — or four times the force of gravity. Simply put, you feel as if you weigh four times as much as you do on the ground, because you are trying to accelerate away from the earth while gravity pulls you back. Internal organs shift, heart rate and blood pressure increase, and blood drains from the head and chest and pools in the hands and feet. Extreme or prolonged positive Gs can cause temporary loss of vision or consciousness. The Earth is always the victor in this tug-of-war, because the plane lacks the power and speed to escape its grasp.

If you draw this circle in a downward trajectory, pushing the aircraft toward the earth, you'll feel negative Gs, or weightlessness. The pressure forces blood into your chest, neck, and head. It feels like a head cold and sinus infection rolled into one and multiplied by ten.

Like any good instructor, Biff prepared my father for the physical challenges of aerobatic flight. He would have stressed the importance of focus. Any lapse in concentration could result in catastrophe.

"*Oscar Zulu* — Wilson Tower," a faraway voice crackled in Dad's headset. "You may begin your manoeuvres at your discretion."

High above the stout tower building, white wings circled lazily like a giant vulture drifting in rising columns of savannah air. Dad's right hand moved smoothly forward, taking the control column as his left hand came back slightly on the throttle. The whisper of the slipstream sliding past the long canopy built its breath to a dull moan. On the instrument panel, one needle crept up as another unwound rapidly. Suddenly, a shadow eclipsed the sunlight streaming into the cockpit. Eyes looked up, a smile creased sunburned skin. A cloud, as soft and pure as driven snow.

A rattle passed through the airframe. Dad muttered an airspeed, his voice barely audible over the hum of the engine and the rising crescendo of the slipstream. Then, a smooth pull on the stick, wings flexing, and the earth fell away underneath the propeller's disc. *Oscar Zulu* bounded upward with vigour and grace.

Up, up, and up. He leaned on the right rudder as the sound of the slipstream faded and gravity kicked in. *Oscar Zulu* continued its upward arc, cresting the top where up is down and down is up, and the pilot felt light in his seat and in his heart. A quick glance down revealed the billowing top of the cloud and the airport below. Sweeping elegantly down the arc's reverse, the engine's hum grew louder, life returned to the stick, and pilot and machine braced. The needles did their familiar dance. A rush of speed, and *Oscar Zulu* swept under the cloud's skirt and out the other end, clawing skyward in a vertical climb. They might never stop accelerating, never stop climbing. Maybe, and only this once, they might escape velocity and break the bonds of gravity.

Alas, the airspeed began to decline. The breath of the slipstream faded and there was an uncanny silence. Dad's left foot moved the rudder pedal to full deflection. Some twenty feet behind him, the rudder responded and the nose was forced left through the pivot. *Oscar Zulu* sliced cleanly through the sky. As Dad hung in his straps, once again falling toward earth, the cloud slid by only inches above his head, its wisps caressing the aircraft's wooden frame.

My dad fell madly in love with aerobatics.

"Pull!" Biff hollered from the back seat. "Pull!"

His voice barely registered over the snarl of the Chipmunk's engine. It had a radio to communicate with other airplanes and ground stations but no intercom. The pilots used a modification of an archaic system known as the Gosport Tube, a device invented in 1917 by pioneering flight instructor Robert Raymond Smith-Barry and named for the location of his flight school. In the Chipmunk's version, the instructor spoke into a mouthpiece attached to a length of rubber hose that ultimately split and led to tiny ear cups inside the student's helmet. It was more effective than tin cans and string, but it allowed only one-way communication.

My dad increased the back pressure on the Chipmunk's control column. It was a last-gasp effort. The plane barely made it past the vertical before running out of energy. Robbed of airspeed and thus lift, the Chipmunk slid backwards for an instant before pointing her nose earthward. The savannah south of Wilson Airport filled the windshield. Reinvigorated by the speed of the dive, life returned to the plane. My dad, his breathing shallow and rapid, tentatively pulled back on the control column and returned the plane to straight and level flight.

Biff reached forward over his instrument panel and clapped a reassuring hand on my dad's shoulder. "Not enough pull. Ran out of airspeed." My dad nodded. "Right." Biff gave his shoulder another squeeze. "Off you go, then."

Dad hauled back on the stick, and the Chipmunk scrambled skyward along the arc of the loop. In the back, Biff flexed his abdominal muscles and thighs in an effort to stem the rush of blood coursing toward his feet.

"Too much," he croaked. But my dad couldn't hear him. He was focussed on getting to the top of the loop without stalling.

The Chipmunk staggered. A tell-tale rattle buffeted the airframe. My dad's training had taught him that this was the airplane warning him that the wings were failing to produce lift and a stall was imminent. A wing only produces lift when air passes over its surface. As the angle at which the wing meets the onrushing air is increased, the wing generates more lift. At a certain point, the air begins to burble and then separates in roiling waves from the surface of the wing, the airfoil stalls, and the plane promptly falls out of the sky.

Dad ignored the warning signs. About a third of the way around the loop, the Chipmunk stalled. The left wing dropped sharply, and the plane rolled neatly around her axis and ended up in a dive, just as before.

"Too much!" Biff hollered into the speaking tube. "Feel the airplane! Listen to her!"

The Chipmunk is a harmonious flyer and a favourite among pilots because of her sweetly balanced controls. Still, she was designed and built when aircraft engineers adhered to a strict credo for trainers. A trainer, they believed, must be easy to fly but difficult to fly *well*. The Chipmunk embodies that principle perfectly. It's why, more than seventy years after her first flight, the Chipmunk is highly prized and much loved. Nearly thirteen hundred were built in the United Kingdom, Canada, and Portugal, and the type remained in service until 1996. Today, about five hundred Chipmunks, a remarkable number, are still flying, and every year, more are hauled out of rubbish heaps and the dark corners of old hangars to be rebuilt and flown again.

My father hauled back on the control column and, as the horizon disappeared, glanced left to keep it in view. They crested the vertical. The Chipmunk settled onto her back, and he released some of the back pressure so that the airplane's momentum carried it gently over the top of the loop. Both men felt lighter in their seats as the horizon reappeared through the glass canopy above them. My dad let the nose fall earthward and pulled back to complete the vertical turn.

"Good," Biff said approvingly from the rear seat. "Again, please."

And so, under Biff's careful guidance, my father waded further into the world of aerobatics. After each manoeuvre, Biff's critique identified an error that, if rectified, would result in the greatest possible improvement. In this manner, the neophyte aerobat grew in confidence and skill.

The beauty of aerobatics is that one lives in pursuit of a perfection that is, of course, unattainable. An aerobatic pilot may perform one hundred versions of the same manoeuvre flawlessly, never be truly satisfied, and then absolutely mangle the hundred and first manoeuvre. The loop, in particular, is exceptionally difficult to execute perfectly. If you were to hand someone a piece of paper and a pencil and ask them to draw a perfect circle, chances are they wouldn't be able to. Flying the perfect loop is infinitely more challenging — so challenging that, if given the choice, even the greatest aerobatic pilots in the world omit the manoeuvre from their routines.

The other major building block of aerobatics is the roll — a 360-degree rotation around the aircraft's longitudinal axis. Every aerobatic manoeuvre has an element of the loop and the roll. They are the foundation upon which the limitless possibility of aerobatics is built. Once my dad had a good grasp of both, a dozen more flights in the Chipmunk, a Beagle Pup, and a Cessna 150 Aerobat followed. Biff moved on to manoeuvres with the exotic names of avalanche (a quick roll at the loop's apex), Immelmann (a half loop followed by a half roll), and hammerhead (a vertical climb with a 180 degree pivot at the apex). With more practice, my dad's confidence and capability grew. Before long, Biff cut him loose to practise on his own. And my father launched himself into the sport with the reckless abandon of a young man, unencumbered by attachments and accountable only to himself.

By April 1973, my father was getting ready to leave the African plains for destinations unknown. Work had either dried up in the equatorial sun or grown stale and boring, so my dad went in search of a new adventure. He repeated this pattern several times throughout his life. His last flight in Africa was a lunchtime half-hour aerobatic jaunt in the RF-5. He abandoned the unfinished airplane he'd been working on in one of the hangars at Wilson Airport. Then he went to Germany, where he spent two weeks in the Hesse town of Bottenhorn in the foothills of the Westerwald mountain range, living the lifestyle of an aerial gypsy. He made a handful of flights in gliders and ferried a Cessna back from Breitscheid before continuing home to San Giacomo.

After three months, there were no suitable job offers — at least nothing that piqued his interest. Then, one day in August, came a knock at the door. Two *carabinieri*, Italian state police, waited with

*As a private in the Italian
Army, December 1973, my
dad wore the insignia of
his regiment, Granatieri
di Sardegna Mechanized
Brigade, on his left sleeve.*

orders to take Antonio F. Rotondo to the nearest military depot. All
Italian citizens were required by law to serve the nation, many of them
through terms in the armed forces. My father had left Italy before
being drafted and could return as long as he didn't stay longer than
three months. He had overstayed his welcome by a week. And with
that, my father became a private in the Italian Army.

At twenty-eight, he was at least five years older than the oldest of
his draftee class, ill-suited to barracks tomfoolery — running around
a field randomly firing a submachine gun for enough money to buy a
Coke and two slices of pizza wasn't exactly his idea of a good time. He
immediately made an appeal to his commanding officer to be transferred to the air force, given that he was an educated man with pilot
training. His captain did the best he could and sent him to Naples to
take a six-month course in becoming a wireless operator.

In Naples, he found the local flying club and, after going up with an instructor to find his bearings, bookended his course in Morse code by flying through his home skies for the first time. In June, he returned to his unit as a *marconista*, or wireless operator, and participated in manoeuvres where he rode around in an armoured personnel carrier festooned with antennae in order to signal the other armoured personnel carriers and tanks in the battalion. He and his fellow wireless operators thought this was great fun until they realized that, should their unit ever be sent into battle, their vehicle would be the first targeted.

Despite the forced nature of their employment and the futility of their actions, these were happy times. My dad recalled that they had little to worry about except to ensure that their boots were polished and their pants were pressed. Gags like exploding shaving cream canisters and swapping out tapes of Morse code signals for the chart-topper of the day were common. They were well-fed, well equipped, and well respected. In those days, a soldier in uniform could hitchhike home, and he often did.

My father was discharged from the army after eighteen months of service. It was the summer of 1975. In August, just a month shy of his thirtieth birthday, he returned to Canada, where he had been offered a job as a concrete forming surveyor, similar to what he had done in Africa, but on more complicated, higher profile projects. My grandmother had moved to Canada just a few months before, and for six months she, Dad, and Uncle Dante lived in my uncle's house on Coronado Court in Toronto's Humbermede neighbourhood. When Dad purchased a small bungalow of his own across the street and Dante married, my grandmother moved in with Dad.

They were very close. My grandmother was an austere woman with a mischievous streak that would occasionally get her into trouble. As a young woman, she played pranks on her sisters. Once she lead her youngest sister outside, saying she had something to show her, and then locked her out. Dad clashed with her on occasion, mostly over her single-mindedness and selective hearing. When challenged, she would respond with a shrug that could be infuriating. Their arguments were legendary, but Dad loved her and defended her tooth and nail because of the support she had given him when he wanted to further his education and travel abroad.

It didn't take long for my dad to seek out an airport to fly again, though in a land dramatically different from the one in which he learned. Dad drove north from Toronto to Collingwood, a town nestled on the shores of Georgian Bay's southern point, pulled into the parking lot at Collingwood Airport, and walked into the offices of the Collingwood Aviation Academy (known as Collingwood Air).

In the mid-seventies, Collingwood Air was a thriving flight school that went out of its way to provide a home for hobby pilots and fledgling professional aviators alike. The school ran a varied fleet of nearly new Piper Cherokees for basic to advanced training, a Cessna 150 Aerobat, and a Bellanca Decathlon for aerobatic and emergency manoeuvre training, and also had access to a variety of aircraft for specialized work. The airport was isolated enough to provide ample airspace for training with very little transit time, yet close enough to the busiest airspace in Canada. Trailers were available for rent if a student wished to stay the night, and the main building was equipped with a shower and a small kitchen. My dad quickly set himself up and began his commercial pilot training.

Since Dad was so familiar with the Cherokee, his license conversion and training went well, and it wasn't long before he was looking for some specialized experience. He found an aerobatic Bellanca Decathlon and convinced Ken Richardson, the chief flight instructor, to go for a spin — quite literally. They likely added a few hammerheads, some Cuban eight work, and an avalanche or two for good measure.

About three weeks later, my dad somehow charmed his way into the pilot's seat of a Chipmunk at the now defunct King City Airport in Vaughan. He no doubt told the owner — likely an Edmund Baklarz of Brampton — that he had flown Chippies in Africa under the tutelage of a former RAF instructor and aerobatic guru, and rhapsodized about how it spun sweetly in one direction while bucking and snapping violently in the other. At any rate, he sweet-talked his way into taking her up solo for nearly two hours.

On August 24, 1976, my dad took off from the nearby Maple Airport in a Piper Cherokee with a Department of Transport examiner in the passenger seat. Two hours later, they landed, and Tony Rotondo became Canada's newest commercial pilot.

My dad had no interest in flying professionally for an airline, however. His pursuit of the commercial pilot's license was rooted in learning, seeking out new challenges and opportunities. The standards for a commercial pilot were higher than those for a private pilot, and the closer attention to precision appealed to him. He also thought that leaving the door open to working as a pilot, even on a part-time basis, was not a bad idea. The company he worked for had projects all over the province and might be interested in hiring my dad and a plane to shuttle men and supplies. At the same time, flying dominated Dad's life outside of work, and he likely thought he could monetize his hobby by becoming a flight instructor and working a few hours a day on weekends. In late June 1979, he began the ground school training for a flight instructor but, in just a week, realized that it wasn't something he thought he'd be very good at or enjoy. He lacked the patience a flight instructor requires. He had flown with many instructors whom he considered the gold standard, and he didn't see enough of them in himself.

The idea of flying into remote lakes and spending the weekend at a cottage did appeal to him, however, and so, in late July, he started float flying lessons on Ontario's Lake St. John near Orillia. On the water, a float plane is more a boat than an aircraft and so the pilot must also be part sailor. Float flying requires specialized training, but many pilots find it appealing because a runway doesn't limit them. They can land almost anywhere, as long as the body of water they've chosen is suitable.

According to his flight log, on August 4, my dad was preparing to leave Orillia on a tour of local lakes to satisfy the cross-country requirement of his float training. On the same day, a pilot named Charlie Miller landed at Orillia in his Smith biplane *Foxtrot Alpha Mike*. This may well have been my dad's first opportunity to get a close look at the airplane he would eventually buy.

Four

In 1965, as my dad was settling into life in Toronto, another young dreamer was falling in love with a biplane in nearby London, Ontario. Larry Butt first saw a Smith Miniplane during a visit to an Experimental Aircraft Association (EAA) fly-in event at Rockford, Illinois, where Don Smith, Frank's son, was showing the prototype Smith and some of the early examples. Butt thought the little biplanes were exciting and now, in a garage on Highbury Avenue, where a man named Robert West was selling his unfinished Smith Miniplane, Butt had a chance to buy his own.

West had already welded the biplane's fuselage and tail surfaces, and they sat on the landing gear. West had also built a set of wings, but Butt wasn't happy with them, regarding them as a "mess." Despite this, and the fact that West wanted a higher price for the project than Larry, just twenty-one years old, recently married, and working in the shipping department of a fuel-additive manufacturing plant, could afford, he saved up, bought it, and trucked it back to his father's place, where he stored the unfinished plane in the garage. He didn't even have a pilot's license yet (he earned his wings about a year later). Larry set about rebuilding the wings to his satisfaction, all the while thinking of the adventures he would have. But sometimes the dream just isn't enough. Time and money were in short supply, and work on the Smith slowed and then stalled altogether. The project became a bitter reminder of a goal left unrealized, and Larry eventually put it up for sale. He found a buyer in Fred A. McGregor, who lived in the small town of Brucefield, Ontario, just a few miles inland of Lake Huron's eastern shore.

In September 1970, McGregor applied to the Department of Transport for registration letters — a call sign — for the Miniplane project he purchased from Larry Butt. At the time, all Canadian aircraft registrations began with *CF*, or *Charlie Foxtrot*. For the balance of the registration, McGregor chose his initials: *FAM* — or *Foxtrot Alpha Mike*. But McGregor never flew the airplane that bore his initials. Instead, he sold it, still unfinished, to a Toronto pilot named Ernst Muller.

Three years later, roughly when my conscripted father was marching around a parade square near Bari, Italy, the low hum of an 85 horsepower Continental engine grew to a growl at a small airfield north of Toronto. A small blue-and-white biplane rolled down the paved runway — tail low, propeller thrashing the autumn air at high revolutions. The tail rose. Both sets of wings began to fly under the rush of air. The button nose swung slightly, and the rudder flicked right, right, left, right to compensate. Galloping down the asphalt runway, wings begging for flight, flying wires flexed, the rigid gear grew fidgety and impatient with the pilot who chose to hold his brave little ship back just a moment more.

No romance, no style, no grace — only a point two thousand feet beyond where the runway vanished at the intersection of green field and deep blue October sky. A barely perceptible bit of aft pressure on the stick, and the runway fell away, and the biplane bounded into the air. Ernst Muller had just left the ground in *FAM* for the very first time. Maple Airport was his Kitty Hawk. On the ground, the Smith was squirrely and kept his feet busy. In the air, however, she was perfect — so light on the controls that he needed only two fingers to guide her through the skies.

His first test flight lasted twenty minutes. Muller deliberately kept that first flight short because he knew the airplane would be tough to set down again — especially on asphalt — not just because she sat

An early photograph of Foxtrot Alpha Mike *in her original colours when owned by Ernie Muller. This shot was likely taken at Maple Airport, north of Toronto, in 1973 or 1974.*

(Photo courtesy of Charlie Miller)

so nose-high that he couldn't see over the nose, but because of her characteristic shiftiness on anything other than grass. That first flight was the culmination of a year of work for Muller. He had finished the airplane in the garage of his Rexdale home. He painted her blue and white with yellow accents, the colours and style of the Experimental Aircraft Association. After getting wet during a rainy flight, he added a canopy. He performed some basic aerobatics, and the plane spun sweetly. He learned that, because of the angle of the fuel tank, she was prone to power loss during takeoff if the fuel level dropped below one-third.

Muller flew the Smith for almost five years. He filled fourteen pages of her logbook and racked up 509.5 hours. The furthest east he took her was St. Lazare, Quebec. The furthest west: Gore Bay on Manitoulin Island. He logged every flight meticulously: date, nature of flight, pilot's name, times up and down, air and flight time, and aircraft total time. In all that time, he didn't set anything down in the remarks section, which suggests to me that he belonged to the camp of pilots who saw their airplanes as merely machines.

⊘

Charlie Miller, *FAM*'s fifth owner, grew up racing motorcycles and boats. An uncle's offer of a flight in a Piper Apache opened up the world of flight, and Charlie was hooked. He started working on a private pilot license, sought out a Bellanca Citabria, and discovered the magic of aerobatics. After his instructor lent him a copy of Richard Bach's *Biplane*, Charlie made up his mind: he must have one.

In the summer of 1978, Charlie was going through one of the most traumatic times of his life: he was nearing thirty, he'd found three grey hairs, and he had a private pilot licence but no airplane. After forlornly chasing the unpredictable summer weather and competing with other pilots to rent airplanes at his local airport, Charlie decided, against all sensible advice, to buy his own machine. His list was short and sweet: it must have two seats, good manoeuvrability, low fuel consumption, and be cheap to operate and maintain.

Charlie looked up newspaper ads and sought out leads. When he found a promising target, he packed his list, a lunch, road maps, and aeronautical charts, fired up his Volkswagen Beetle, and chased down the prospect. Day by day, trip by trip, Charlie considered and rejected prospects. The Pitts S-2 gulped fuel. The Chipmunk and Mudry CAP 10 were too pricey. Charlie was faced with a blank page and an empty heart. He needed more money. Everything in Charlie's world went up for sale: $500 for his camera, $10 for a hockey stick, $20 for a tape recorder. Snow tires? Sold.

When his second car, a BMW sports coupe Charlie had rebuilt

himself, drove off with its new owner, Charlie had accumulated $9,385.78 of flying money.

Charlie knew Ernie Muller from local Experimental Aircraft Association meetings. He had no idea Muller had an airplane of his own, let alone a Smith. He didn't even know what a Smith was. At one meeting, they happened to be sitting next to each other and chatted as they waited for the meeting to begin. Charlie mentioned that he was looking for an airplane and told Muller about his list.

"Have I got the plane for you!" Muller exclaimed, eyes shining. He pulled out his wallet and thrust pictures of *FAM* into Charlie's hands. The plane wasn't officially for sale, but Muller was working on another project. Why didn't Charlie drop by King City Airport and have a look? If he liked it, Muller said, a deal could certainly be worked out.

Charlie immediately fell in love with Muller's biplane. More than three decades later he still remembers *FAM* "as the prettiest little blue-and-white Smith Miniplane you ever saw." This was the biplane he'd dreamed of since the day he picked up Richard Bach's book. But would his six-foot frame fit inside the diminutive cockpit? As soon as he slipped into *FAM*'s single seat for the first time, he knew — and Ernie Muller had a deal. Charlie doesn't remember exactly what he paid for *FAM*, only that it would prove to be worth every penny and more.

After a quick pep talk from Muller, Charlie fired up the engine, opened the throttle, and watched helplessly as the little biplane promptly turned in a complete circle. It would be his first lesson in the biplane's notoriously cantankerous ground-handling characteristics. "There are two kinds of airplanes — those you fly and those that fly you," the aviator Ernest Gann astutely observed in his memoir *Fate is the Hunter*. "You must have a distinct understanding at the very start as to who is the boss."

There were a few more failed attempts and a raised eyebrow from *FAM*'s soon-to-be former owner before Charlie surrendered the pilot's seat. Muller flew the Smith one last time, a trip to Brampton. Charlie followed in Muller's car, peering up through the windshield in a vain attempt to keep an eye on his prized airplane.

Charlie spent a week getting to know the plane without leaving the ground. He ran *FAM* up and down Brampton's runways: first slowly, with the tail down, then a little faster, endeavouring to raise the tail-wheel and bring life to the stubby twin wings. Each practice run was a conversation between plane and pilot, a lesson in what the aviator must do and when. In a single seat aircraft, no instructor, no seasoned veteran, guides you. The airplane, therefore, becomes the teacher, but the pilot must remain the master. It is a delicate proposition, one balanced precariously — in this case, on rigid Taylorcraft landing gear.

After a week of tentative courtship, Charlie and *Foxtrot Alpha Mike* left the ground together for the first time. "It was a learning experience," Charlie says now. "Very exciting lessons taught between two short wings and a total lack of forward visibility."

The Smith was everything he'd dreamed of: quick, manoeuvrable, and exciting. After each pulse-racing flight, however, Miller returned to find his girlfriend waiting. Not long after, and thanks to Ernest Muller once again, Charlie bought a two-seat red-and-white Aeronca Champion, and *FAM* had her first stablemate.

But change was in the air. The leaves turned from green to red, orange, and yellow. The humidity drained from the southern Ontario skies. The air grew cool and fresh and then cold and sharp.

Charlie took *FAM* apart, storing the fuselage in the garage of his Bramalea townhome and the wings in the living room. He'd insulated the garage door against the ferocity of Ontario's winters, but he still found it cold, especially when he had to open the door to go in and out. One day, an accidental but conveniently placed hammer strike opened a hole in the garage wall. Charlie could see into a closet on the other side. In short order, he installed a door on the inside of the closet, giving him access to his airplane without going outside.

Charlie reshaped the sheet metal coverings surrounding the cockpit and engine. He created new coverings for the landing gear legs, found a new spinner, and reshaped the nose bowl. He used a rubber hose covered in Naugahyde to trim the cockpit opening, and installed a new instrument panel, complete with a G-meter for aerobatics. He repainted *FAM* in the iconic red-and-white colour scheme of the Pitts Special biplanes, which he considered the biplane's visual ideal. To the top of each wing, he applied six ice-white lines spreading out from the centre like the rays of a rising sun. Four smaller lines graced the top of the tail's horizontal stabilizer, and he painted a broad white band down each side from the end of the engine cowling to the tip of the tail. The aircraft's wheel-pant fairings were similarly adorned. The little biplane wore these colours for the rest of her flying life.

In the spring, he moved the pieces of his plane back to the Brampton airport and reassembled them in the EAA's hangar. When his good friend Gordon Skerratt bought a Smith Miniplane of his own, Charlie had his dream biplane, a wingman, and a vast sky in which to indulge his imagination and fly in make-believe dogfights.

The land beneath *FAM*'s twin wings was arid brown and yellow. The day was oppressive. The sun's heat felt vindictive, and the air was heavy and thick. The hills seemed to roil and swell. Every few miles, an old farm drifted past.

Charlie had spent the better part of the day trying to stay awake: mouth agape, eyes staring dumbly and unfocussed, sweat dribbling down his forehead. He'd been anxious to get off the ground, but in the cockpit aloft, there was little respite from the heat. Even the wind shoved back from the propeller thrashing against the thin air was hot. The hum of the engine and subtle vibration of his machine threatened to lull him to sleep. He took desperate gulps of the hot air, hoping they might revive him.

He noticed a barely perceptible change in the engine's drone. He knew something was amiss. A quick scan of the sparse instrumentation revealed the mixture-control knob as the most likely culprit. In his heat-induced stupor he must have brushed his sleeve against it and drawn it out farther than it needed to be. He leaned forward to adjust it, happy to have a commonplace duty to focus his attention on, even briefly.

He felt the bone-jarring hammer blows of the twin Spandau machine gun before he heard them. The mixture control was quickly forgotten. He instinctively slammed the stick one way and pushed the opposite rudder to the floor. The horizon abandoned all reason and spun around madly. The sound of the slipstream changed in tone as the wind strummed the flying wires. Charlie's stomach turned.

He looked through a neat hole punched in the upper-right corner of the biplane's windshield. From its borders, tiny hairline cracks splayed out like beams from the day's harsh sun. He'd never before seen such a perfect circle. He would have marvelled at its beauty and simplicity if not for the fact that, had he not leaned aside to adjust the mixture, the bullet that created that hole would have buried itself below his right eye.

Charlie jerked his head around. His silk scarf billowed out behind him as the flaps from his leather helmet fluttered against his cheeks. Another biplane was turning around below and behind his own ship. It had cream-coloured wings with red stripes and a crimson nose bowl. He recognised it instantly as the mount belonging to a rival ace.

Charlie pushed the throttle through the gate and smoothly pulled back and to the left on the stick. His biplane slowed as it approached inverted, and he added enough rudder to bring the nose around. His target hovered below him now, clawing his way skyward in a climbing turn. Charlie let the nose drop through the horizon and rolled hard to the right.

Suddenly, the cream-and-crimson biplane sat in the middle of Charlie's windscreen. His wings, however, were set at a sharp angle, and it was immediately obvious that he was approaching at a great velocity. Charlie had but an instant to strike.

He felt the airplane shudder and slow as he fired the Vickers machine guns. The smell of cordite filled the cockpit and dust speckled his goggles. His opponent flashed by over the top wing, engine snarling in defiance. He pulled back hard and arced high to the left, tilting his head back to catch a glimpse of his quarry. Charlie's skin was on fire with the heat and slick with sweat but his insides were ice cold. The longer the jousting match continued, the greater the odds that Charlie's opponent would emerge the victor. He had to end it quickly.

Charlie's last manoeuvre was more aggressive. He gave his target another two-second blast from the Vickers. The result was devastating. Angry tongues of flame licked at his cowls. Thick black smoke spewed from the engine, billowing between the wings and wires and obscuring the cockpit.

The handsome little biplane steepened her roll toward Charlie, who pulled back on the stick and rose above his victory. He watched her slide underneath and roll onto her back. She dove out of view.

His eyes caught a shade of movement on the right wingtip. Charlie rolled sharply toward the new target. The biplane's speed increased and the rush of air intensified. The dot floating in the middle of the windshield sprouted two wings and a tail. As he continued his approach, it grew larger. Charlie hunched his shoulders, flexed his fingers around the control column, and heard his heart thumping in his head.

This target was one of the new monoplanes. He was cruising leisurely and very much alone. He was so close that Charlie could easily see where the fabric around the exhaust stacks had darkened with heat and grime. He could have counted every rib pushing against the red fabric. Below the cockpit rim was a stencilled name and a small patch of fabric covering some recent damage. The rigger had yet to paint it to match the rest of the ship.

Charlie triggered the Vickers guns. He heard a metallic clang, but no bullets emerged. Jammed.

Charlie hauled back on the stick, and his biplane rushed upward.

He felt the monoplane slide beneath them. He tilted his head back and saw that he'd betrayed his approach. The other pilot was now very much aware of Charlie's presence and manoeuvring to gain the advantage. Charlie rolled out to face him, and they rushed head on toward each other.

Charlie broke away hard, up and to his left. The horizon tilted crazily and slipped out of view, and he pulled the airplane into a near vertical bank. Charlie's opponent zipped past. The muzzles of his twin Spandau flashed, and an instant later Charlie heard and felt bullets whizzing past him. The monoplane roared overhead, and Charlie yanked back on the stick and bounded upward to follow.

This deadly dance continued for what seemed an eternity but may have been mere minutes. Charlie's new opponent was an old and skilled hand. There were no wasted movements. Each act was calculated and deliberate, yet executed so swiftly Charlie had the impression his opponent wasn't thinking at all but running purely on instinct. It became evident that the outcome of this meeting would depend not on who was more skilled, but rather on who would commit the first error.

That fell to Charlie. He pulled too hard in an effort to latch onto his opponent's tail. His biplane wallowed right then snapped her left wing down hard and tumbled into a spin. He reacted instinctively and snapped out of the spin as quickly as the biplane fell into it. Still, it was too late. As Charlie pulled out of the dive, his opponent's bullets were spiralling between the wings and through the flying wires.

His opponent may have been faster, more skilled, and able to both out-dive and out-climb Charlie, but few planes could out-turn his biplane. And so, with the bullets careening around him, Charlie swept into an ever-tightening left turn. As they raced around this crazed carousel, Charlie wondered if he was merely delaying the inevitable. His guns, after all, had jammed. He couldn't mount an attack of any kind. To cut and run would have meant certain death. Outside of waiting for his opponent to run out of ammunition, fuel, or patience, Charlie could do little but keep turning. His opponent could not score a hit without tightening his turn, and he could not tighten his turn without stalling. They were at an impasse.

After a few minutes, on one of his frantic glances rearward, Charlie noticed his hunter had disappeared. Charlie levelled his wings to discover his opponent flying alongside. His rival pulled his goggles away from his eyes to reveal a jovial grin on an oil-streaked face. He raised a gauntlet in salute, waggled his wings, and started a sweeping turn to the west.

It was time to go home.

Charlie closed the throttle and let the speed spill from the wings. The earth rose up to meet him, and he levelled off just above the countryside. The landing was uneventful. Charlie taxied to his tie-down and switched off the engine. All the other airplanes were already in their spots. He was the last to return.

Despite the setting sun, it was still very warm, and Charlie was in a hurry to get out of the airplane. He pulled off his goggles and damp leather helmet and hung them on the intersecting flying wires to his left. He ran a hand through his dark hair, matted with sweat, and smoothed out his moustache. Taking a deep breath, Charlie wrapped his gloved hands around the cabane struts and pulled.

Minutes later, he pushed his way into a crowded tavern. The barman gave him a grin and nodded toward the far corner where a table was laden with pub fare. There were puddles of beer everywhere. Crowded around the table were the other pilots, still clad in leather flying jackets and oil-stained coveralls.

"So, there I was, hanging in my straps, and Roy comes up from behind..."

"I swear I had the son of a bitch, and next thing I know, he's on my tail..."

"...out of airspeed, out of ideas, and staring God in the face... I thought I was a goner, for sure..."

Charlie's first opponent from the evening's aerial joust was sitting across the table. He pushed a glistening pint of ale across to Charlie.

"Bottoms up, Charlie," Gord said. His airplane was just fine and tied down a short drive away. The bullets, smoke, and flame were imaginary. The victory, however, was very real.

At the other end of the table, George Jones, their local Experimental Aircraft Association president, recounted how he came to be Roy Hems's victim. George excitedly described the mock dogfight with his hands. Roy, who actually flew Spitfires in the Second World War, sipped his beer and silently said a prayer of thanks that today's battle was fought with their imaginations.

A few seats away, George Welsh, another Second World War Spitfire pilot, was deep in conversation with another combatant. Charlie made eye contact, and George, his face still dark with oil, gave him the same grin he'd flashed from the cockpit of the monoplane not an hour ago. Charlie raised his glass in salute.

And so it went, once a week, all summer long. At a predetermined time, EAA airplanes would meet over the Caledon Hills north of Toronto, and every pilot would be on the lookout for an attack from any side. Some guys even called in sick to get out to the airport early and stake the best chance to "bounce" an opponent. There were no guns, so a "kill" would be scored once the aggressor pilot latched onto an opponent's tail. A head-on attack or a strike from the side would not count. From the ground, it must been quite a sight: a cloud of colourful airplanes tangling like gnats, buzzing as they looped, rolled, yanked, and banked around the summer sky.

These were the "Brampton Boys," a ragtag collection of airmen flying an eclectic mix of homebuilts and old classics. Spitfire veterans Hems and Welsh flew Bowers Fly Baby monoplanes, and Bunny Lamoureux piloted a Monnett Sonerai II racer. Charlie, Gord, and George Jones were Smith biplane pilots. Other members flew Aeronca Champions, Cessna 140s, Piper Cubs, Volksplanes, and even a Pietenpol Air Camper, a parasol monoplane that first took to the skies in 1928.

Charlie Miller flew Foxtrot Alpha Mike *almost daily.*
(Photo courtesy of Charlie Miller)

In the seventies and eighties, Brampton was a hotbed of home-building activity and home to what remains one of Canada's busiest general aviation airports. And Charlie flew the Miniplane almost daily: cross-country trips into small grass fields, formation flying, aerobatics. He even flew in winter, dressing as warmly as he could and heating the engine oil in a kettle on the stove before driving out to the airport. It could be twenty below, but he'd pour in the heated oil and the engine would come to life like it was July.

Charlie and Gord loved getting lost. One of their favourite things to do was to blast over the countryside in their Smiths, not overly concerned about their precise location. At least one of them had a map, but it wasn't much use. Maps are next to impossible to read in an open-cockpit biplane, and most of Ontario looks the same, so there's no guarantee you actually are where you think you are. Charlie's preferred way of navigating, provided he could nail down his location, was to moisten his thumb and press it against the chart. It left a telltale mark that would survive for about five minutes in the summer heat. By the time it evaporated, he knew he was about five minutes from where he'd started and therefore not that lost after all.

One hot summer afternoon, Charlie and Gord flew out over Muskoka. There was no breeze to speak of, and the sky was so hazy they couldn't pick out any landmark to navigate by. And the higher they climbed, the worse it got. A mat of green hills and shimmering lakes spread out below. If the compass could be trusted, however, Charlie was fairly certain they were heading south.

And then, the sunlight's reflection off the surface of a particular lake caught his eye. Every other lake shone a blinding white — hot, flat, and featureless. This one lake seemed to dance, like the ripples on a puddle. Charlie waggled *FAM*'s wings and glanced back at Gord, flying in formation mere feet away. Charlie pointed to his own eyes before jabbing a gloved finger downward: *Look down there, and follow me.*

With the throttles pulled back, engines nearly idling, the two biplanes made a silent approach. Charlie and Gord dropped over the trees at the lake's northern end and right down to the surface before throttling up for the final seconds of the approach. They realized what was causing the ripples they had seen at altitude: a canoe, rocking slowly back and forth. Two legs stuck up and out of the canoe, with something round and white between them. The startled, naked couple frantically tried to keep the canoe from capsizing as the two biplanes roared overhead.

Clearly, they were still in cottage country.

Charlie owned *Foxtrot Alpha Mike* for only three years, but he logged nearly three hundred and fifty hours in its single cockpit. Later he and Gord went on to own and fly Stampe biplanes. They even lived as barnstormers for a time, visiting local airfields and taking people up for rides. Charlie designed, built, and flew a long list of interesting airplanes, ultimately becoming one of the world's foremost builders and

Charlie Miller in Foxtrot Alpha Mike *(right) and Gord Skerratt in* Romeo Echo Bravo *(left) blast across the front yard of Gord's Tottenham home as the dogs look on.*

(Photograph courtesy of Charlie Miller)

restorers of Bücker Jungmanns and Jungmeisters, aerobatic biplane trainers of the 1930s German Luftwaffe. His "steel and wood children," as he terms them, now fly across the skies of Canada, the United States, and Europe. It all started, however, with *Foxtrot Alpha Mike* in the endless blue of Ontario skies.

Charlie kept an extensive pictorial record of his time as *FAM*'s pilot and caretaker. In one, Charlie does his best impression of the Red Baron. In another, Charlie and Gord's biplanes are less than a wingspan above the earth and separated by about thirty feet, blasting across the front yard of Gord's Tottenham home — and over their respective dogs. In today's era of tightly controlled airspace, highly travelled airways, glass cockpits, urban sprawl, and crowded skies, it is hard to believe just how recently pilots like Charlie and Gord flew free, jockeying for position and glory, rattling the windows of Gord's country home. They revelled in the rush of speed, the exhilaration of the wind rushing through the cockpit and along the fabric flanks, the surreal sensation of gravity's pull and lift's might — the magic of flight.

Five

As Dad approached his mid-thirties, his dark hair started to thin. He put on a little weight. He grew a giant handlebar mustache, mostly as a joke to see if he could, and then shaved it off in favour of a full beard, dark brown and flecked with gray and red. It did little to hide the easy grin and the twinkling eyes. Life was good: he liked his job, he owned his own home, and he had enough money in the bank to indulge in his hobbies.

Work consumed him. His colleagues were his friends. He met the man who would become my godfather, Alberto Chioran, an Argentine-Canadian, when they were paired together to do the survey work for Wonder Mountain at Canada's Wonderland, an amusement park. Alberto became one of his best friends. Work intensified when Dad was moved to the huge Harbour Square project in Toronto. He kept up with judo and learned yoga as a way to stay fit and help relax. He dated very little. Any free time was spent flying.

Having a commercial pilot's license meant that he could combine his two passions: work and flying. His employer had a pair of projects in northern Ontario and realized that moving men by small airplane was faster and more cost-effective than using the company van. Plus, the men arrived at work better rested and with more time to work. The company hired Dad to make a few trips. During one such flight, he made a mistake that nearly cost him his life.

He had just left Sudbury in a four-seat Piper Warrior, a larger, more powerful version of the airplane he'd learned to fly in. He'd taken a heading of roughly south and was looking at a distance of about fifty miles before he'd reach the northern shore of Georgian Bay and then another eighty over the water to Wiarton. He'd already made a two-hour run from Kapuskasing to Timmins and then to Sudbury earlier in the day. The day before, he'd spent nearly four hours in the air, flying first to Kapuskasing and stopping to drop off men and gear in Sudbury and then Timmins. He'd considered skirting the eastern shore of the bay, but bad weather was on the way, and that was the long way around. The weather would be on top of him before he got to Wiarton. Back at the terminal in Sudbury, an old man had looked up from his newspaper and warned my dad not to go.

Wind whipped the trees and water below. Georgian Bay stretched out beyond the nose and crystalline arc of the propeller. On either side, clouds billowed and broiled, building into ugly masses that choked the horizon. Rain began to speckle the windshield. The wind picked up. The whitecaps on the lake grew larger.

Fear in an airplane is a lonely and unforgiving thing. It is cold. You shiver and sweat. The numbing drone of the engine is no longer a comfort but a constant reminder of your isolation and insignificance. Every decision made up until this point becomes both meaningless and monumental. You are willing to make any number of deals and bargains to whatever power you think might help you survive. Fear whispers in your ear and breathes on the back of your neck.

The horizon disappeared. Everything was a uniform gunmetal blue. There was neither up nor down. He might have been in cloud; he might not. He realized the bottom was falling out. Another five or ten miles, and his flying days could be over.

My dad looked hard at the instruments. He was truly, deeply scared. He regretted not listening to the old man at the terminal. Then he drew on his training: he made a 180-degree turn and got the hell out of there. Thirty minutes later, the little Piper touched down in Sudbury. Dad climbed out carefully and walked slowly through the rain, letting the drops wash away his fright. The old man was still in the terminal building, reading his newspaper.

The experience didn't deter Dad from flying. Rather, it pushed him to do more. He began looking for an airplane of his own that he could fly whenever he felt like it. He didn't have anything specific in mind, but something simple, an easy flyer that was affordable to operate and maintain, would be fine. A plane that could be the starting point for a story, unique and eye-catching, would be better.

My dad found *FAM* in the simplest and most traditional way — by answering a classified advertisement. It was April 1981. Charlie had put the Miniplane up for sale and took out an ad in the *Toronto Star*. Charlie still loved the Smith. It was the first airplane he'd ever owned and the first one he'd worked on to truly make it his. But he was looking for something with two seats to take people for rides. Another airplane, a Belgian-designed biplane known as a Stampe, had caught his eye.

They met at the Brampton airport, and Dad did the usual things involved in the acquisition of a plane: he examined the airplane and the logbooks, sat in the cockpit, plucked flying wires, and strummed fabric. The airplane oozed cool. Though it wasn't fast, it looked it — even parked on the ground. He imagined the freedom it would give him. This was the airplane of his childhood dreams. It hadn't been long since Charlie was in my dad's shoes. He knew exactly what was going through his mind. Looking at the silly grin on my dad's face, Charlie felt lost and forlorn. Memories of his great adventures with Gord came flooding back, and Charlie fought hard against changing his mind about selling. Instead, he took the airplane out for a few laps of the airport while my dad watched. When Charlie landed, he and my dad shook hands on the deal, and *FAM* had a new pilot. Dad had used most of what he'd earned in Africa to buy his first home. But he still had a decent sum left over, and paid Charlie's asking price of $8,000 on the spot. Dad couldn't contain his excitement. He owned his own airplane! Charlie was certain that Dad would have paid more for it, if he'd asked. At the time, selling that plane was the hardest thing Charlie had ever done.

Dad was neither confident nor foolish enough to try to fly the Smith up to Collingwood himself, so Ken Richardson, Collingwood Air's chief pilot, flew the biplane to her new base. It took him more than an hour and a half, despite the fact that the distance between airports is a little more than forty miles — barely a half hour in the Smith. Presumably, Richardson succumbed to the little biplane's charms and indulged himself. When he landed at Collingwood, an aviation mechanic looked the airplane over once more — just in case.

Dad's plane sat idle at Collingwood for nearly two months while he tinkered with his new toy. He changed the throttle from the traditional left side to the right to mirror the setup he was most comfortable with. He also installed a different tailwheel assembly to improve visibility over the nose. He repaired a few spots on the fuselage where the paint had worn away and exposed the fabric underneath. He carefully sanded away the flakes of paint, cleaned the area, and then applied dope, a coating made of cellulose dissolved in acid, which protected the fabric and tightened it around the airplane's body. When it dried, he painted over the repairs with cherry-red paint and buffed *FAM*'s coat to a rosy glow. The minor tweaks drove him nuts. He yearned to fly her.

What's the best way to learn to fly a single-seat plane? The most widely favoured is to practise taxiing at various speeds on all three wheels and also on the front wheels alone. The rationale is that, before leaving the ground, you must be able to handle your craft through the critical phases of takeoff and landing, which the high-speed taxi simulates. The second method is to pick a calm day and a wide, quiet field, open the throttle and raise the tail, and just fly the plane. Airplanes, after all, are designed for flight and make terrible ground vehicles. Dad's training and his disposition dictated caution. Like Charlie Miller and Ernest Muller before him, my dad used the first approach, practising taxiing the biplane up and down Collingwood's grass strip, first at low speed with the tail down, then at higher speed with the tail up and running on the main wheels.

At three o'clock one June afternoon, he impulsively decided to leave the ground.

He felt only the air's whisper against his brow. The whine of the engine labouring inches behind the Spartan instrumentation drowned out all other sound. His right hand rested on the throttle. His left moved forward, and the tail obeyed, lifting the tailwheel off the grass.

Through the cabanes and down the button nose, he saw the end of the field first inch and then gallop toward him. Muscle memory dictated that the right hand move aft, and then, once the rush of speed subsided, he should lower the tail and be ready on the rudder pedals.

Hidden in the wind's whisper was a scream that cut through the mechanical moan of the engine and the concentration of the pilot.

Let's go.

The wheels left the ground. The next forty minutes were for plane and pilot alone. The cockpit is a sanctuary. Solitude isn't for everyone, but it has certain benefits.

Emboldened, the next day he spent the three-and-a-half hours doing circuits, and for the month that followed he flew the plane as much as he could, in and out of small airfields dotting the landscape to the south of Collingwood — Lake Simcoe, Meaford, Maple, and King City.

The Smith brought together everything my dad loved about flying. It was a taildragger that challenged him, kept him on his toes. And it turned heads; people wanted to have a closer look everywhere he went. But what Dad loved most was *FAM*'s single seat. It meant that every minute of every adventure would be his and his alone. Flying solo is what my father valued most. The Smith gave him that.

TURBULENCE

Six

Like my father, my mother, Anna, was born in Italy, but she grew up on the other side of the world. In 1950, just a few months past her first birthday, she and my grandmother set sail on the *Tucuman*, a former US Navy Victory ship, bound for Argentina; my grandfather, a cobbler, had gone ahead to Buenos Aires a year earlier, shortly before my mother's birth, hoping to establish himself before his family followed.

The *Tucuman* left Sicily and stopped at Las Palmas on the island of Gran Canaria off the coast of Africa, before continuing to Buenos Aires. My grandmother fell ill a few days out of Las Palmas and remained in the sick bay for the duration of the thirty-one day trip. A woman from the Argentine province of Mendoza looked after my mother during the voyage. On one occasion, while using the bathroom, she left Mom on the other side of the stall door rather than bringing her inside. My mom, fourteen months old, stood up and toddled off along a passageway, seemingly retracing her way to the sick bay by memory. When my mother's caretaker, frantic at having lost her, arrived in the sick bay to tell my grandmother what had happened, she found Mom curled up next to her mother in her bed.

Mom's father took a job in a shoe factory in Buenos Aires. He saved up and bought a house and opened his own shoe store in the nearby city of Quilmes, where the chief industry was beer brewing. As a little girl, my mom ran errands on her own, taking the bus into the capital to buy supplies for my grandfather's shop — about a thirty-minute ride. She disembarked on Patricios Street and visited three wholesalers (to this day she remembers their names: Vartaberian, Churukian, and

Casa Juancito) who had shops in the same block, buying about thirty pairs of shoes and paying with money hidden in her own shoes. Mom then took the tram back to her home in Quilmes. It took twice as long as the bus, but there was more room for the packages of shoes, which weren't very heavy but were large and awkward. The errands would take four hours, most of the morning, and she did this a few times a month. My mom found out years later that her father followed her for the first few trips to be sure she was safe.

When Mom was nine, her sister, Cristina, was born, a month premature and weighing less than four pounds. She was the only girl born in the clinic that day, and my grandmother didn't come home with her for almost two weeks. Once she did, she cloistered herself in the bedroom and cared for my aunt for months, leaving only to use the bathroom and to take the baby to the doctor in the neighbouring block about once a week. Mom ran the household, cooking and cleaning while my grandfather minded the shop. She went to school only in the afternoons and did her homework at night. She remained at the top of her class and had the honour of carrying the Argentine flag in the country's independence day parades.

It took nine months for my aunt to recover from her premature birth, and was finally baptized on my mom's tenth birthday. A beautiful baby with blonde curls, she wore a dress of light pink lace and white shoes that threatened to fall off her tiny feet. My mom remembers a feeling of relief that life would return to normal.

Like many men of his day, my grandfather didn't believe his daughter needed an education beyond elementary school but would most benefit from a job. So at age thirteen, my mom began training as a seamstress. During the day, my mom worked in a small upstairs room, making dresses, skirts, and blouses for clients. At night, and in secret, she completed high school, studying accounting, typing, business courses, and English. She graduated when she was eighteen.

In January 1968, my mom was hired as an administrative worker at a financial services company, and for the next six years she worked in a variety of accounting jobs in banks, at a printing company, and at the largest manufacturer of industrial machinery in South America. Her mother's two younger brothers had emigrated from Italy to Canada in the early 1960s, and in 1973 my grandmother paid them a visit. It was the first time she had seen her brothers in more than twenty years. When she returned to Argentina, she and my grandfather decided their family would also move to Canada, to be close to my grandmother's family and take advantage of better opportunities for my mother and my aunt. The plan was that my mother would immigrate first, and her parents and younger sister would follow her a few years later.

Mom, now a tall, slender young woman with pale skin, red hair, and freckles, arrived in Canada in 1974. One of her uncles helped her land a job in the service department of a car dealership in Ottawa. She lived with him, his wife, and their three daughters in a small two-storey home near Ottawa's Experimental Farm. Except for a brief visit by her father, my mother didn't see her family again until 1977, when she returned to Argentina for a visit. In the meantime, a military dictatorship had gripped the country and terrorized its people. The Ezeiza International Airport in Buenos Aires teemed with soldiers toting submachine guns. A customs official seized her Argentinian documents and sequestered her in an interrogation room. Opposite her sat an army officer at a desk, hammering away at a typewriter. Three soldiers flanked him. Every so often, the officer would glance up at Mom, spit out a question, and, once he had an answer, resume typing. She felt as though she was being treated as a criminal, and was so frightened she blocked most of the event from her memory. She doesn't remember what she was asked or how she answered.

The minutes ticked by while her father, waiting in arrivals, grew increasingly concerned. Her flight had arrived nearly two hours earlier, and still no sign of her. Fortunately, a family friend worked at the airport as a maintenance employee, and my grandfather asked him to see if he could find my mother. He found her in the interrogation room. Not surprisingly, the soldiers refused to allow Mom to leave with him.

The clack of the typewriter keys stopped abruptly. The officer pulled the form free, rose slightly in his seat, and leaned across the desk, brusquely thrusting the triplicate form into my mother's hands with a demand that she sign it. She scribbled her signature without even reading it, and she was free to leave. Only after, safely in my grandfather's car on their way home to Quilmes, did she read the form. She had to leave Argentina within the next thirty days or risk detention. Right-wing death squads hunted down anyone who was, or was even suspected of being, a political dissident, a loose term that included not only militants and activists but also students, writers, trade unionists, journalists, and people who had left the country and returned — like my mother.

The political repression notwithstanding, her family's plans had changed. The reason was simple: the country's government would not allow any citizen emigrating to take anything with them. My grandparents would have to leave behind everything they had worked so hard to build: the house, the business, their savings. They would be allowed to leave Argentina with little more than the clothes on their backs and whatever possessions they could squeeze into a suitcase. Having started over with nothing once before, my grandparents lacked the stomach to do it again. They wanted to stay in Argentina, and they hoped my mom would too. A great aunt, however, urged her to return to Canada. The government cars slowly threading through the streets of Quilmes with the windows rolled down just far enough to reveal the barrel of a submachine gun made up her mind. She left again within the week, using her Italian passport to return to Ottawa. While she would return in 1980 and again with my father in 1982, it would take a decade — long after the military junta had relinquished power — for my mother to feel safe in the town she grew up in. To this day, she continues to travel with both her Canadian and Italian passports, just in case.

My mom's early years in Canada were a daze. She spoke Spanish, but her uncle and aunt spoke Italian. Her younger cousins, at least, spoke English, which made it easier to introduce her to the local landscape and Canadian culture. But she had no trouble finding work as a bookkeeper and accountant, first in car dealerships and later for a law firm, and she became a citizen and got her own apartment. Still, she felt she needed the guidance of Argentine ex-pats who better understood where she came from.

She joined a social club for Argentine-Canadians and made many friends. Friends from work taught her to play tennis, and she signed up for Italian literature classes at Carleton University, where she helped found a club for students interested in Italian culture. She also took up ballet and gymnastics. At the gymnastics class she met and quickly became friends with a woman named Susan Richardson.

One January night, Mom and Susan went out for dinner. They had planned to go to a pizzeria downtown, but ended up driving to another restaurant in the south end of the city. As soon as they'd finished eating, Susan suddenly remembered that she had promised to pick up her boyfriend from a friend's place nearby. She had trouble finding the house in question: it was dark, there were no street lights, and the house was newly built and lacked the address number. Only when she spotted her boyfriend's car in the laneway could she identify it. Obviously, Mom realized, Susan's boyfriend didn't need a ride, and this whole thing was an elaborate ruse to introduce her to his friend. She insisted on waiting in the car while Susan went inside.

My mom was wearing a silk dress, a fur coat, and a pair of leather shoes. But she sat in the January cold for half an hour before knocking on the door of the house — she was that stubborn. A man, covered in paint and holding a cup of coffee in one hand, opened the door. He invited her in, offered her coffee, and when she didn't seem all that keen on conversing (she was fuming mad at Susan), he suggested she might like to read a book. He handed her a copy of *Helter Skelter*. It was an inauspicious meeting.

⊘

The previous summer my father had moved to Ottawa to manage the construction of a new Westin hotel. He was reluctant to leave Toronto, but the company he worked for had just finished a high-profile project, and it was a good opportunity. Because he'd be in Ottawa for at least the next two years, he decided to take his plane with him.

At the time, my dad had relatively few hours of flight time — about three hundred — but it had been a varied and eclectic apprenticeship. This flight would be an entirely new challenge. He was no stranger to challenging cross-country flying, but until now he had only taken the Smith out for short jaunts across a far more populated and forgiving countryside. This trip would span nearly three hundred miles in an airplane he had only recently taught himself to fly.

He spent a week poring over charts and seeking the advice of other pilots. He'd make the trip in three stages: Collingwood to King City, King City to Carp, west of Ottawa, and then a hop to Rockcliffe. He left his bungalow in the care of my grandmother. The Smith stayed for a week in Carp while he arranged a permanent home for her at Rockcliffe Airport.

Rockcliffe Airport has a long and proud history. The first landings here were made in 1918, when the land was an army rifle range. Royal Air Force aircraft hauling mail on experimental runs used the land behind the range butts as an improvised landing ground. In 1920, it became the Ottawa Air Station, one of the six original airfields opened by the Canadian government. In March 1930, Billy Barker, a Victoria Cross recipient and one of the country's great aces of the First World War, died in a fatal crash at Rockcliffe. Four years after the solo flight that made him an icon of aviation, Charles Lindbergh stopped at Rockcliffe during a northern survey flight with his wife, Anne Morrow. (She chronicled this flight in her book *North to the Orient*.) During the Second World War, it was an important training base and in the post-war years launched many flights to map the North.

My dad with his Smith at Rockcliffe Airport in the spring of 1982.

Dad promptly joined the Rockcliffe Flying Club and his unique little biplane attracted a lot of attention. It wasn't long before he had made friends and connections at the historic airport, including Susan's boyfriend, Xavier.

And Susan was nothing if not determined. On Valentine's Day, she invited my mom to her place for dinner and promised that only Xavier would be joining them. When Mom arrived, Dad was there too. It was a long, quiet dinner, after which my mom asked Susan to call her a taxi. My dad insisted he'd drive her home; after some prodding, my mom agreed. The trouble was my dad had illegally parked and his truck had been towed away during dinner. Susan lent them her own car. My mom, still miffed over her friend's unwanted matchmaking, hardly spoke on the drive home, and got out of the car without a word. But Dad made up his mind that he'd keep trying.

On a Sunday morning a few weeks later, Susan convinced my mom to go with her to church, despite the fact that neither woman was much of a church-goer. During the drive, Susan confessed that she and her boyfriend were not getting along and that she wanted my mom's advice on the matter. But instead of a church, Mom found herself in the parking lot of the Rockcliffe Flying Club.

"No," Mom said.

"Let's go," Susan insisted. "It'll be fun."

Mom's only other option was to stay in the car. Reluctantly, she followed Susan.

Out on the flight line, Dad and his friend were preparing an airplane, a four-seat Beech Sundowner, for flight.

"Okay, girls," Dad exclaimed as he finished checking the oil. "Let's go to Montreal for coffee!"

"In this?" my mom asked, nodding toward the airplane. Susan jabbed her in the side.

They flew to Les Cèdres, an airport just off the island of Montreal, had coffee, and hopped back into the airplane for the return flight. Susan asked my dad if she could ride up front so that she could "fix things" with Xavier. Dad was only comfortable in a small plane if he had direct access to the controls, having been in the backseat of a Cessna during a near-accident in Africa, but he happily gave up his seat and climbed into the back with Mom.

Susan and Mom had plans to see the documentary film *From Mao to Mozart* later that week, but Susan suddenly realized she'd double-booked herself and suggested Dad go in her place. Before Mom could open her mouth to object, Dad happily agreed. He picked her up on the night of the screening. She wouldn't let him pay for her ticket. He fell asleep in the first fifteen minutes. Mom nudged him awake once the credits rolled, at which point he declared he was famished and asked if she'd like to join him for dinner at a smoked-meat joint down the street. She agreed.

In the more intimate setting of the restaurant, Mom softened somewhat. Dad was a good-looking, charming guy. The reserve of his childhood was gone. He smiled easily and had a good sense of humour. He spoke English perfectly — only the occasional incorrect stressing of a syllable in words like *comfortable* and *vegetable* gave him away. He had a weakness for watches and fountain pens, and he liked good food and nice clothes, but he drove a company pickup truck and could swear like a sailor. His disinterest in anything that wasn't aviation- or construction-related was apparent. Several other dates followed.

Dad suggested that Mom learn to fly so that she could be his co-pilot on a flight to Argentina. My mom expressed some doubt that my conservative grandfather would be impressed.

"No problem," my dad said, pulling a pocket planner out of his jacket. "We'll get married."

My mom just looked at him, aghast.

"What do you think of September?" he asked, jabbing a finger at the calendar. "I like the number eleven. And it's our custom that I get a ring, too," he added.

Keeping up her end of the bargain, my mom enrolled at a flying school at the Ottawa airport, did the ground school, and started taking lessons. The lessons went well, but clearly Dad's Miniplane couldn't carry them both to Argentina. My parents spent $27,000 on a fast four-seat cruiser known as a Mooney M20E, built in 1964, that Dad found through the aviation classifieds. He had five grand saved, and Mom scraped together ten. Mom had a mentor who offered to loan them the remaining twelve thousand. They picked the plane up in Gimli, Manitoba, in July and flew it back to Rockcliffe. It was a high-performance Mooney — clean, fast, and built like a tank.

The plan, as ambitious as it was foolhardy, was to fly it south to Buenos Aires. It would be their honeymoon. My dad bought the charts and started mapping it out. Three decades later, the maps survive. If you pull them out, it's easy to see the would-be adventure's evolution and how my dad's enthusiasm faded as his doubt swelled. Over Central America and the northern part of South America the notations grow sparse. He's scrawled question marks over lakes and towns. There simply was too much water, too much jungle, too much political upheaval, too few airports, and too many places and ways to die.

My parents married on September 11, 1982. Rather than fly their Mooney south, they chose a comfortable ride on a Pan American Clipper.

They enjoyed a meandering honeymoon: Caracas, Venezuela, followed by a week on Margarita Island in the Caribbean and then a week in Rio de Janeiro before continuing south to Argentina, where they stayed for ten days. My grandparents did more than accept my dad — they loved him like a son. Having lost his own father, he grew particularly attached to my grandfather. Dad spoke to him in Italian, and because my grandmother had lost hers, he learned Spanish from my aunt. She would sit on the couch and give my dad words and phrases that he, lying on the floor with his hands folded behind his head, dutifully recited. Like English and Swahili before, he learned to speak the language so well that one could hardly tell he wasn't a native speaker.

My parents on their wedding day.

My parents returned to Ottawa in the middle of October, and their new life together soon found a familiar rhythm. Dad continued working on the Westin Hotel project while Mom remained at the law firm. Weekends were spent flying the Mooney together: to Montreal for coffee or lunch, over the Laurentian Mountains to Mont Tremblant for the day, or simply short flights to other airports around Ottawa. The Mooney could take them anywhere they wanted to go quickly and comfortably. But the Smith remained my dad's favourite. Flights in her were low, slow, noisy, and windy affairs, but she was always fun. And, as my dad would say, a twinkle in his eye, "Wherever you went, you did it in style."

This was the world I was born into in November 1983. My parents, fittingly, named me after Jonathan Livingston Seagull, the character in Richard Bach's novella. Bach's story of a young seagull who, unfulfilled with a life of squabbling over food scraps, embarks on

When I was nine months old, I took my first flight — an eighteen-hour trip to visit my grandparents, aunt, and uncle in Argentina. Here I am with Dad on the ferry at Carlos Paz in the fall of 1984.

learning everything about flying was not only required reading for pilots in the seventies and eighties but also enjoyed enormous popularity outside aviation circles, and inspired much New Age self-reflection. Cast out of his flock, Jonathan becomes increasingly skilled, learning to travel great distances in little time and reaching another plane of existence before eventually returning to teach other outcasts.

My mom's flying lessons ended when she learned she was pregnant with me, and my parents stopped flying the Mooney together after I was born. My dad flew the Smith regularly — about twice a week through the spring, summer, and fall — until the end of 1985. That September he went into business for himself, founding a concrete-forming company. My sister, Vanessa, was born in November. These two events changed his outlook. He now had two children and a wife who stayed home to care for them. Having struck out on his own professionally doubled the pressure. Getting the company off the ground was hard work. Dad was the president, project estimator, and general manager. Things were lean at first, but my dad's skill as an estimator helped him outbid larger, established companies for projects, mainly apartment blocks, office buildings, and bridges. The hours were long and he routinely came home after dark. Mom handled the company's books while taking care of us and all the domestic duties. Dad often took me with him to work to give Mom some space, but she put a stop to it once I started picking up some of the colourful job-site language.

Despite the long hours, the stress, and the pressure, Dad still tried to find time to fly his biplane. If there was still enough light out after dinner, he rushed off to the airport to fly a few circuits. My mom washed the dishes and put us to bed. I'm sure she resented it at times, but she also knew how important flying was to him. Sometimes, he returned just in time to read us a story or give us a goodnight kiss. Then he poured a cup of coffee or a small glass of wine, retreated to his drafting table in the basement, and went back to work. In the dim light of a lamp, he pored over structural plans until midnight.

Inevitably, the flights began to dwindle, and he no longer record-ed them in the Smith's logbook. These hours and minutes now seem particularly special: they were his alone, existing only in his mind and heart. Eventually, *FAM* sat idle.

Dad often arrived home exhausted. Naps after dinner were com-mon. I remember watching his chest rise and fall and, for some reason, worrying about what I would do if this breath was his last. In the same vein, I would kneel on the couch that backed onto the large front window of my childhood home and wait for his car to pull into the driveway. Sometimes, I would walk out to the end of the driveway and wait for headlights to appear the end of the street then hurry back inside, hoping those two beams of light would illuminate the house rather than continue past.

My dad had a brilliant mind, but he wasn't a businessman. He started his own business because he didn't like being told what to do, and he thought he would do better for himself on his own. But my dad was too nice. He hired friends and people he knew and then felt obliged to pay them more than he could afford. And he trusted people more easily than he should have and refused to believe that they would betray him. Whenever faced with making a difficult decision that might adversely affect others, my father put himself in their shoes and considered the impact his actions or words might have on them. His company began to falter. Dad sold the Mooney. Then he sold *FAM* to another pilot at Rockcliffe. He kept this to himself. My mom found out only when the new owner knocked on our door to return toys I'd left in the cockpit during one of my pretend flights. He took a loss on both planes. In 1990, the company went bankrupt, and so did our family.

Two events are burned into my memory. The first is my mom, in tears, confronting my dad about a bounced cheque. I knew what a cheque was, and I couldn't understand how a piece of paper could bounce and why she'd be so upset if it did. I also remember sitting in Dad's deserted company office, on one of those hideous, over-stuffed, scratchy tweed office chairs that seemed to be everywhere in the eighties — my legs dangling. My sister sat on our mother's lap. My mother was refusing to sign over ownership of the house to my dad. She insisted that the house remain separate from the assets of the company and thus protected from bankruptcy. My dad kicked a partition so hard it nearly toppled over. And then, in a voice so calm that even thirty years later it still makes me shiver, he reminded my mother that he'd built the house: it predated both her and us. Mom signed the papers, and we lost the house.

Desperate to minimize the impact of all this on me and my sister, my parents rented the house my father had built. Mom went to work on the overnight shift in the mailroom at Canada Post. Her shift began at eleven in the evening and ended at seven the next morning. She would tuck us in, grab a quick nap, and then head to work. In the morning, Dad would meet her outside the front door with a cup of coffee before he left for work. Mom would draw a bath and fall asleep in the tub. The cooling water woke her. She prepared breakfast, got us ready for school, and then ran errands and did the housework. Then she returned to the law firm and worked days. She slept only for a half hour in the morning and for a few hours after dinner. Dad would take us to the corner store for freezies or to the park so we could run around. Mom was awake again by the time we returned home. Somehow, she worked those two jobs for eighteen months. My mom, though exhausted, was toughness personified. She alone pulled our family out of the hole my father had dug.

Dad was a shadow of his former self. He went back to work for a former boss putting together project bids; he was paid $100 a week. And when my mom returned to work, the cloud he lived under only grew darker. In his mind, he'd failed himself and his family. He was humiliated. It would be years before he touched the controls of a plane again.

When I was not quite eleven and my sister not quite nine, my dad received an offer to work for a Toronto-based construction company running several high-profile, innovative projects across North America. The position was in Vancouver, and it paid well. This was the chance he was waiting for, and he took it.

Other kids' parents were married and living together or were divorced. Vanessa and I existed on some island in between those two states. I found it embarrassing and tiresome to try to explain our situation. My parents' marriage grew strained, and my relationship with my sister changed too. In my father's absence, I felt I had to grow up. I felt pressure to not only fulfill the responsibilities of an older brother but some of the fatherly duties as well. When Vanessa didn't like one of Mom's decisions, she'd lash out, and I would step in. She didn't appreciate my efforts to get her in line.

Vanessa and I are quite different. She inherited our dad's aptitude for math and science, earning a bachelor of science. And she's also musically gifted. From our mother, she inherited toughness. She recently triumphed over an extremely aggressive breast cancer, facing it down with the strength and determination that Mom displayed during our family's toughest times.

Growing up, we dealt with the stress in very different ways. Vanessa felt she had to buy flowers for Mom on her birthdays and anniversaries and fix things around the house. She couldn't understand why Dad couldn't just call a florist himself, why the only responsibilities that seemed to matter to him involved his work. And yet Vanessa stood by Dad in disputes, while I tended to side with Mom. She and Mom fought a lot, and the two of us resented each other for taking adversarial positions. When Dad was away, the tension left with him, but Vanessa's anger remained, and it affected her for years. I felt pressured to become more adult, and she rebelled: lousy friends, drugs, excessive drinking, and partying.

Dad worked out of town for fifteen years — first Vancouver, then Toronto, Niagara Falls, San Diego, and finally Calgary. He returned home one weekend a month. Dad was present in parts of my life and notably absent from others. He taught me to drive stick shift and explained how and when to change out the furnace air filter. It was a neighbour, however, who taught me how to barbecue great burgers and the best way to grill chicken breast to ensure it didn't dry out. When he was home, my father was more of a guest than a resident. He couldn't remember what cupboard the mugs were kept in and which drawer held the silverware. He couldn't be bothered to hang a picture or fix a leaky faucet. As soon as he crossed the threshold and set foot in the house, he seemed preoccupied by the job he'd only just left. Airports, once places of fun, promise, and adventure, meant only that he was leaving us again.

Seven

When I was a baby, my parents would pack me, a basket of food, and a lawn mower into their pickup truck and make the drive to Rockcliffe. I'd sit in the Miniplane while my parents cut the grass. Then my mom would pull me out, and my dad would hand swing the propeller to fire her up. He'd jump in and head out for a local flight or some circuits. We ate lunch and watched and waited for him to return.

Later, after Vanessa was born, we spent our weekends visiting airports or chasing hot-air balloons. The latter involved spotting a balloon, piling into the family car, and quite literally chasing it to discover where it would land. It seems absurd now. But for my six-year-old self and four-year-old sister, it was an adventure. Every weekend was.

Dad could charm his way onto any airport ramp simply by telling a story, dropping a name, or waving his tattered pilot's license at a dispatcher. And then, with us in tow, he'd glide up and down the flight line telling us about each airplane. If a door was unlocked — and they often were — Dad would load us into the pilot and co-pilot seats and snap a few pictures while Vanessa and I pretended we were flying over the Amazonian jungle or crossing an ocean. We flew thousands of miles across many eras — with Lindbergh across the Atlantic and with Earhart and Noonan on their tragic attempt to circumnavigate the globe — without ever leaving the ground.

The Canada Aviation Museum (now known as the Canada Aviation and Space Museum), then housed in three surplus Second World War hangars on Rockcliffe's southern aprons, was another almost weekly destination. Here, airplanes from the Great War to the jet age sat

My sister, Vanessa, and I with a Teenie Two homebuilt monoplane
at Carp Airport, near Ottawa, in 1989.

under one roof as if they had only just returned from a flight. Here, a little boy could walk under the wings of a mighty DC-3 airliner that had blazed new routes in the infancy of commercial air travel, delivered paratroopers behind enemy lines during the Second World War, dusted crops in Louisiana, and shuttled rock stars on tour. Not far away at Carp Airport, another frequent stop, a pack of them still plied their trade with the company that eventually became First Air. Under this roof, the Spitfire shared space with her mortal enemy, the Messerschmitt Bf 109. In the shadow of George "Buzz" Beurling's bronze bust, Dad taught me about the famous Canadian Spitfire ace who had shot down more than thirty enemy aircraft in the Second World War and then, unable to adjust to civilian life, volunteered to fly with the Israeli Air Force, only to die in a plane crash in Rome in 1948. In another corner stood a Chipmunk that prompted my dad to tell us about learning to fly aerobatics with Biff. As long as there were airplanes, Dad had stories. We could see the joy it brought him to share his love of flight with us.

We would drive out to the end of the runways at the Ottawa Macdonald-Cartier International Airport to watch the airliners take off and land. They passed so low I felt as though I could reach out my hand and touch them. The sound they made, even at low power on approach, was both exhilarating and frightening — an earth-shaking roar that you felt in your chest rather than heard with your ears. In airport terminals, I was the kid with his nose pressed up against the glass, completely absorbed in watching the arrivals and departures.

My dad was a voracious reader, and while his tastes were varied and sometimes questionable, his overflowing bookshelves held many treasures. I read everything that had an airplane on the cover. Before I was ten, I could identify by sight most military airplanes and a good many of their civilian counterparts. I knew a fair amount about Second World War military aviation, could rattle off the top five air aces from each side on command, and could make a compelling argument for why the Hurricane was more important than the Spitfire during the Battle of Britain. Dad taught me about aviation pioneers such as Charles Lindbergh, Amelia Earhart, Pancho Barnes, Jackie Cochran, Chuck Yeager, Art Scholl, and Bob Hoover. He spoke as if he had known them, and so I felt as if I knew them too. When most kids my age worshipped hockey and soccer stars, I idolized aviators. They were my dad's heroes, and they became mine.

My first flight in a small airplane came on a May weekend in 1990 when I wasn't quite seven years old. We waited nearly all day in line at a community fly day for a twenty-minute ride in a four-seat Cessna. My sister whined and fidgeted, begging for Dad to pick her up. I stood next to him quietly, my legs aching. All I cared about, all I could see through the sea of legs ahead of me, was the little green-and-white plane waiting for us on the other side of the fence.

When the time finally came, my dad sat in the back with Vanessa. I rode in the right seat next to the pilot. After we levelled off above the city, the pilot let me take over. I could barely see over the instrument panel, but the control wheel felt good in my hands. One tilt of the wings was all it took: I made up my mind that I would be a pilot.

Despite my upbringing, aviation was in some respects an odd choice, the countless hours I spent "flying" Dad's Smith notwithstanding. Almost abnormally risk-averse, I was not an adventurous child. I was far more comfortable in a library than on a sports field. Climb a tree or a piece of playground equipment? That meant begging for a fall.

I got my first bicycle — a gift from my godfather — for my seventh birthday. He drove it down from Toronto in the middle of a snowstorm: a Raleigh mountain bike in cherry red. I still remember how the foam handlebar grips shrunk under my hands and then slowly returned to their original form when I let go. It looked so new, sleek, and fast.

However, there was six inches of snow on the ground, and the mercury was moving in the wrong direction.

The bike was also far too big for me.

And I didn't know how to ride it.

My parents put it in the basement for the winter. You would think that would deter me, and normally you would be right. Still, something about that bike goaded me and challenged me. Even standing still it looked fast. It begged to be ridden.

One afternoon, I popped the kickstand back, hoping no one would hear the sharp sound it made, and rolled it into the basement family room. The spokes clicked softly. I leaned the Raleigh up against the couch. Taking a deep breath, I climbed onto the couch and then onto the bike. With a firm push off with my left foot, I took off across the basement, pedalling furiously and wobbling like a drunk as I dodged the coffee table. I crashed a few seconds later into the loveseat.

I undertook a few more such journeys before the snow melted and my parents found a bike more my size for ten bucks at a nearby garage sale. It was navy blue and at least ten years old, with stainless steel mudguards dented by falls and pockmarked by rust. When the wheels turned, they sounded like a corroded cheese grater. My dad had at least pumped the tires, greased the chain, and added a pair of training wheels.

For days, I rode it up and down the driveway. I didn't even try turns. I just hammered the brakes, skittered to a stop, dismounted, dragged the bike around, hopped on again, and aimed for the garage door.

When I finally mustered the courage to try a turn, I eased the huge, curved handlebars to the right and leaned my body into the turn. The bike balanced precariously on one training wheel. I'll never forget the sound: like kicking a jar full of nuts and bolts down a curved staircase.

But now the world was open to me. I began riding farther and farther. Each ride was an adventure from which I returned older, wiser, emboldened.

One fine summer's day, the right training wheel decided it had had enough and abandoned its post. The bike and I teetered back to my driveway, either balanced awkwardly on the main wheels or listing heavily to port. Two days later, the remaining training wheel failed. It did, however, have the decency to cling grimly to the axle, clattering along in my wake.

I was at least a quarter mile from the safety of my driveway. I found that the faster I pedalled, the easier it was to stay balanced and run straight. More to the point, the bike was easier to control at higher speeds, needing only the slightest of touches on those oversized handle bars. And so, I set my sights on my destination and, with the sun in my eyes and the wind in my hair, enjoyed the journey. Now I look back on these early forays into cycling and realize flying, particularly in an open cockpit, is very similar: the relation between speed and balance, the promise of adventure, the excitement of discovery, and the sense of accomplishment.

❂

I was about eight years old when I decided I wanted to fly fighter planes. My parents had given Vanessa and me an old IBM 286 for Christmas, bought second-hand from a family friend who had loaded some of the first-ever flight simulators onto the hard drive. I spent hours in the soft glow of the computer screen, flying Spitfires during the Battle of Britain and a top-secret American stealth fighter on sweeps deep behind enemy lines. But in the seventh grade I noticed it was becoming difficult for me to read the chalkboard in class, and soon I was wearing glasses for my short-sightedness. At the time, the Royal Canadian Air Force accepted only pilot candidates with perfect vision. My dream of becoming a military flyer went down in flames.

I could still become a pilot, however, and at thirteen I joined the Royal Canadian Air Cadets. The cadet program had been founded during the Second World War to train young men for military service and, by the time I arrived in the fall of 1997, it had evolved to focus on leadership, citizenship, and physical fitness while promoting an interest in aviation and the Canadian Forces. One night each week, our squadron gathered for parade night. We learned the basics of drill: how to stand at attention, salute, and march singly or in large groups. We were issued uniforms and taught how to care for them. Weekends were reserved for special events, including survival exercises. Flying days, in either airplanes or gliders, happened twice a year. This was the first taste of flight for many cadets.

Cadets interested in eventually earning a license and their wings faced a long and difficult road. Cadets in large squadrons, like mine, had to advance through three increasingly complex levels of ground school. Generally held on weekends, these classes focussed on theory of flight, engines, navigation, weather, and the laws of the air. Younger cadets who did well in the lower levels could earn a place in a two-week summer course meant as a pre-license primer. Sixteen-year-olds could apply for a glider pilot scholarship, and seventeen-year-olds could throw their hat into the ring for the private pilot license to fly powered airplanes.

Competition for these summer courses was fierce. Only three hundred scholarships were available across Canada each year, and thousands of kids participated in the program. Each squadron, depending on its size and past performance, could put forward only one to three cadets to compete. Candidates then had to score well on a notoriously difficult regional exam and submit to a gruelling panel interview.

I worked hard and consistently placed at or near the top of my class in each level of ground school, but the summer I was first eligible for the pre-license course, my parents took us to Argentina to visit Mom's family. In the next two summers, I wasn't chosen to compete for a glider scholarship. I was also passed over twice for the power pilot scholarship. I just couldn't seem to do enough to get myself noticed. In June 2001, seventeen years old and having endured four consecutive rejections, I decided to quit.

I carefully cut the badges from my uniform which I then pressed, folded, and placed in a garbage bag along with my boots and wedge cap. I planned to return it all to my squadron quartermaster on our final parade night of the year. With the exception of skating lessons when I was barely three, I hadn't quit anything in my life. My parents had taught me to finish what I started, but I had taken this as far as I could — or so I believed. Dan Hutter, a school friend of mine and a member of a squadron across town, dropped by and asked about the bag. He urged me not to give up without visiting his unit first, which was meeting the next evening.

I joined the new, smaller unit and fit in extremely well. My new squadron did not have a formal ground school program, and so our small group of hopefuls prepared under the guidance of one of our staff members. We read textbooks deep into the night until we could scarcely keep our eyes open. We dug reams of old regional exams out of the squadron supply locker and wrote them all several times. When we ran out of exams, we created our own, and we conducted mock interviews.

That spring, the regional exams and interviews were held in the school at the old Rockcliffe air base. I polished my boots to a mirror shine and starched the collar of my uniform shirt until it was stiff as a board. Of the fifty questions on the exam, I missed only two. I felt like I'd impressed the interview panel as well.

Three months later, I hit the refresh button on the Air Cadet League of Canada's website, as I'd done every hour for the last two weeks. That morning, a list of names cascaded down the screen. I scrolled to the bottom of the page, counted up from the bottom, and read the names aloud. When I reached nine, I read the name *Rotondo, Jonathan D.* It took a moment for me to realize that the name was my own. Of the 300 scholarships awarded that year, number 291 was mine.

As far as aerodromes go, Les Cèdres Airport didn't look like much. The airport was sandwiched between the highway on the south and a yard where they auctioned off wrecked cars, bloody interiors and all, to the north. The three-thousand-foot runway wasn't in the greatest shape, but the school we would train with, Laurentide Aviation, had a long and proud history of training pilots in Canada. Founded in 1946 by former Royal Canadian Air Force pilot Jack Scholefield, Laurentide originally opened up shop at the now-closed Cartierville Airport. In 1970, it opened its own airport at Les Cèdres where it remains a family-owned business.

We piled out of the van and let our duffle bags fall to the asphalt. I felt a mix of anticipation, excitement, fear, and pride. Our instructors, clad in crisp white shirts and black pants, stood in a line before us. The planes that would be our mounts waited on the other side of the perimeter fence. A tall man with thinning gray hair atop a head inclined ever so slightly forward introduced himself as Roger Joanette, our chief pilot. He assigned us to our instructors in groups of three or four.

The assignments were made by weight. We soon discovered why: to keep costs down, the school used two-seat Cessna 152s rather than the larger 172s that could carry more weight. The four heaviest cadets, myself included, were assigned to instructor Nigel Barber, of average height but powerfully built, dark skinned, and stern. At twenty-two, he was the youngest instructor. When outside, he always wore Maui Jim sunglasses. He wore a tie, even in 40°C heat and somehow never sweated. He also never smiled. The three other cadets in my group had completed the glider course the summer before. With me, Nigel was starting from scratch. I had studied, and I was familiar with planes, but I had no practical flight training. Even guiding the aircraft to the runway was a challenge, because steering with my feet was an alien concept.

My first flight, like my father's, covered basic attitudes and movements: how to use the control wheel to lift and lower the nose and therefore climb and descend, and how to tilt the wings and begin a turn. My left hand squeezed the control yoke in a white-knuckled grip and my right, trembling slightly, sat on the throttle, which I pushed forward or pulled back to increase or decrease power. Once I'd mastered the basics, Nigel expanded on climbing, diving, turning, and the relationship between power, airspeed, and altitude. He introduced me to the stall and the spin. Back at the airport, we worked on takeoffs and landings.

In military fashion, our days were strictly regimented. We were housed at a recreational camp about ten minutes from the airfield. We had a television without cable and a DVD player without DVDs, but we did have a pool and sand volleyball court. Six days a week, we rose with the sun and were at the airport shortly after seven. We ate all our meals in the café above the flight school. We alternated: half our group flew while the other took ground school classes. If we lost a training day to weather, we made it up on Sunday.

The training was rigorous and risky. We were competitive and jealously guarded the details of our flights. Just days into our course, a cadet flying out of the Quebec City airport froze on the controls. The instructor couldn't overcome the cadet's death grip on the control column, and the aircraft crashed into a newly seeded cornfield, nearly breaking in two. Somehow they escaped injury.

We were required to fly a plane on our own by our fourteenth hour of training and earn our license in no more than forty-eight hours of flight time or risk being booted out of the course. As the first solo tests neared, the circuit around the airfield became busier. It wasn't unusual to see five or six airplanes circling at any given time.

My own first solo came just before lunch on July 3. We started the day practising takeoffs and landings. After about an hour, Nigel asked me to make the next one a full stop and had me taxi clear of the runway at the midpoint of the strip, perhaps two thousand feet away from the fuel pumps. He switched off the engine.

We sat in silence for a moment.

"If you're thinking of pushing the airplane all the way back to the pumps," I said, "you'll have to do it without me." He ignored my comment.

"Do you think you're ready to go solo?" Nigel asked.

"Do you think I'm ready?"

"Yes."

"Okay," I said, nodding. "Okay, I'll go."

"All right," he said, clapping me on the back. "One circuit and then bring her back. You'll be okay." He gave my shoulder an encouraging squeeze, slammed the door closed, and backed away. I gave him a wave, and he flashed me a thumbs-up.

The takeoff was surprisingly short. As soon as the wheels left the ground, I belted out a joyous whoop and aimed the nose at the heavens. I felt entirely free. Everything that happened within the cockpit was honestly and truly only mine. For the first time, I was in command, the plane an extension of my body, no matter how clumsy. I wondered if I would spend the rest of my life aloft, trying to find this moment of communion again. Only when I reached the end of the downwind leg did I fully realize that I had to return both the plane and myself to earth. My descent toward the runway was smooth. I called out my airspeed, throttle, and flap settings to myself, whistling nervously in between each check. As I turned onto the final approach to land, I instinctively glanced to my right. Nigel wasn't there to save me from myself.

I touched down on the main wheels with a little too much speed and rose into the air again. I tried again, and this time the little Cessna stayed on the runway. I taxied to the fuel pumps, where my mates were waiting for me. As soon as I'd switched off the engine, they pulled me from the plane and doused me in the customary ice-cold water.

After the first solo, my flight training continued as a mix of solo practice and dual instruction under Nigel's watchful eye. In an airplane, Nigel was a taskmaster. Transport Canada, a higher authority than our instructor, allowed a margin of error when holding an altitude, heading, or airspeed. Nigel did not. Allowing the compass needle to wander as much as a degree from our assigned heading was an affront. If he noticed that we had picked up an extra twenty feet of altitude in a turn, he accused us of "flying all over the sky."

I came to realize that I was not a natural pilot. I was clumsy and, at least early on in my training, lacked the requisite feel. I was also not a technically inclined person and struggled to wrap my head around much of the engineering and physics side of aviation. I may have flown solo successfully, but I was still uncomfortable with stalls, spins, and landing with a crosswind. But I improved and my confidence grew.

Nigel loosened up and a friendship began to form. I loved flying with him. He never took the controls away from me in flight. If he saw me making a mistake, he would point out the error and tell me how to fix it. Nigel understood that the best way to turn us into safe and capable pilots was to demand exactness in everything. By the end of my training, I was convinced he was either blessed with a total absence of nerves or he was more than a little crazy. When he strapped into an aircraft with a neophyte and patiently and incrementally forged them into a safe pilot, he risked his life. He did not teach the bare minimum. Rather, he exposed us to the limits and capabilities of our airplanes in case we should ever need them. He showed us what it was like to fly in cloud. He drilled us in the steeper turns that we could use when forty-five-degree banks would not free us from danger. He taught us manoeuvres that we'd need for more advanced licenses and ratings. Years later, when I began teaching, I routinely heard his words in the instructions I gave to my own students. After my parents, he was the best teacher I'd ever had.

The sense of competition between the cadets also faded. We missed each other when we went home for twenty-four-hour weekend visits (I went home twice) and were glad to reunite on Sunday evenings.

Halfway through our training, a Super Chipmunk, a modified version of the air force trainer my dad flew with Biff Hamilton in Nairobi, dropped into Les Cèdres for fuel. I took a break from studying to have a look and speak with the pilot and his passenger.

The airplane was impressive: a bold, red-and-white paint scheme with sleek, spatted wheels and an aggressively styled nose. It was a bit of a Frankenstein's monster: the pilot had totally redesigned and rebuilt the fuselage before mating it to a set of wings and a tail section from an original Chipmunk. He'd replaced the 145 horsepower Gipsy Major motor of the type my dad had flown behind with a much larger 210 horsepower engine to give it better aerobatic performance. The Super Chipmunk took off, came around again to give us a low pass, and headed west for Rockcliffe.

Two weeks later, the pilot and a passenger took off from Salaberry-de-Valleyfield Aerodrome, on the opposite shore of the St. Lawrence and only a few miles away from Les Cèdres, for a short aerobatic demonstration flight. After a loop and a roll, the pilot performed a manoeuvre known as a Lomcovák, where the airplane tumbles randomly around all three axes. The Super Chipmunk emerged from the tumble in a spin, but the pilot recovered and began to pull out of the dive. Then, just as the nose began to rise, the right wing separated from the fuselage and fluttered away. With only one wing, the plane was doomed. It rolled multiple times, crashed, and burst into flames, killing both men. The investigation revealed that the pilot, unable to find original bolts to attach the wings to the fuselage, unwittingly used bolts that were similar but weaker. When he tried to pull out of his final dive, the bolts were stressed to the point that they failed. The news of the crash hit us like a punch to the gut. Teenagers think they're invincible. Our group of fledgling aviators was no different, at least until that day. The death of the two men served as a cruel introduction to the dangers we faced aloft. It was a chilling lesson.

By the first week of August, after roughly forty-five hours of flying, a written exam, and a practical flight test, we were awarded our licenses. A few days later, we packed up our belongings and again boarded a bus for Saint-Jean-sur-Richelieu where, on a sweltering afternoon, a major pinned a set of enamel wings onto my chest. I burst into tears. I was eighteen years old and had finally earned what I had desperately coveted for as long as I could remember — it was my greatest accomplishment. My parents, sister, my godfather, and his wife were in the front row. Tears — followed by a fit of uncontrollable laughter — seemed an appropriate response.

Nigel was one of the first people I hugged as soon as we were dismissed from the parade square. I found my family, my godfather, and his wife outside. Mom still had tears in her eyes. Dad was happy and proud but bewildered by the military pomp and ceremony of the event, so different from his own experience at Wilken Aviation: the pipes and drums, the bellowed commands, the swish and gunshot-like report of three hundred cadets turning in unison. We were given literal wings of gold and silver braid to wear on our uniforms.

I continued to fly out of Les Cèdres for a few months. My mom was my first passenger. I took her up in the same plane I had first flown solo in. My dad came up with me about a month later in a different Cessna 152 that could be best described as cantankerous and clapped out. Dad hadn't touched the controls of an airplane in nearly fifteen years, but he made her dance across the sky. He taught me how to fly coordination manoeuvres like lazy-eights and chandelles (a climbing,

180-degree turn so called because the airplane follows a trajectory akin to the flame of a candle). I'll never forget the feel of the airplane in my hands and the sound of the slipstream as we rushed up the arc of a wingover then slid down to earth again. We spent more than an hour and a half carving through the skies west of Les Cèdres, and yet it felt like mere heartbeats had passed from takeoff to touchdown.

I returned to Rockcliffe as a newly minted pilot in the late fall and spent what little money I had renting airplanes. I flew every few weeks: taking friends for rides, practising takeoffs and landings, and flying short cross-country trips with my dad. On one trip, a quick jaunt west to the old air force base at Arnprior, Dad insisted as soon as he sat in the cockpit, that he had flown this particular airplane before, when he learned to fly float planes in Orillia some thirty years earlier. Cessna rolled out the first four-seat Cessna 172 in 1956, and by 2015 had built a staggering forty-four thousand — more than any other aircraft in history. The odds that he was right were, frankly, astronomical. When we returned home, his logbook proved him right. I meticulously recorded each of these flights in my own logbook, and the hours and my experience grew.

The next summer, aged nineteen, I worked with my dad as a surveyor's apprentice on job sites across Ontario. Working with my dad was an eye-opening experience. Not only was he highly experienced — having worked in the industry for four decades — but he was obsessed with reinventing himself to stay ahead of the curve. He constantly took courses to learn how to use the latest technology and then lobbied his employer hard to acquire the equipment. He was in high demand as a brilliant bid estimator and layout man.

But he could be difficult to get along with. He demanded excellence and razor-sharp precision. Errors were unacceptable; a centimetre off on a wall footing could mean having to make up an inch somewhere else in the structure, sometimes weeks later. If the assistant was capable, they were worth their weight in gold, and my dad could be a patient and generous teacher. If his assigned helper didn't exhibit the qualities he was looking for, the apprenticeship would be short, cruel, and laced in expletives. Both my sister and I filled that role for several summers, and we were not spared because we were his children. Dad, despite having quit smoking years before, always had an unlit cigarette between his lips and a spare tucked behind his ear. If we ever saw the cigarette come out of his mouth, we knew to expect a fusillade of cursing, almost always before we realized we'd made an error.

We worked six days a week, often in excess of ten hours a day, burning in the sun and sweating over structural plans. Sunday was our reward. We would rent an airplane, pick an airport, and go exploring. In an airplane, my dad was a different guy. The confines of the cockpit gave him peace and focus.

That first summer working together, we flew Piper Warriors out of the St. Catharines Flying Club. At the time, an outfit called Air Combat Canada had an operation at the airport and my dad insisted I try aerobatics. I went up for an hour with ex-Canadian Forces CF-18 pilot Paul "Pitch" Molnar in a Super Decathlon. I made it all the way through to inverted spins — a sort of upside-down descending cork-screw — before I threw up. But we'd be on the hook for the whole fee even if I asked to end the flight early, so I closed the airsickness bag and finished the flight. When I returned to the ground I was forever changed.

The next summer, we flew a Piper 180 out of Canadian Flight Academy at Oshawa. We flew into Collingwood — my dad's first time back in about fifteen years. He didn't say much, but I could tell it moved him to return to the little airport he loved so much and where he had spent so much of his time. Less than a week later, we drove to Newmarket so that I could try flying a taildragger for the first time.

As we pulled into the gravel parking lot at Holland Landing Airpark, I expressed a little doubt. It was a hazy day, hot and humid. The runway was short and bordered by a cliff on one side and a highly travelled road on the other. I had about a hundred hours total time in my logbook and all of it in tricycle gear aircraft designed to land themselves.

"Just wait till you lift the tail," he said. "You'll love it." As I walked to the plane he yelled after me, "Keep moving your feet!"

It was good advice.

I remember I was pleasantly surprised by how much room I had in the front seat. My left hand felt at home on the throttle as I flexed my right hand around the control column. I wriggled in my seat and pushed forward against my straps as I craned my neck over the nose. Holland Landing's runway was the shortest I'd ever seen.

Instructor John Greer was in the back seat. I was reasonably sure he couldn't see a thing. At his prompting, my left hand advanced the throttle smoothly as I added forward stick. The engine responded immediately. With my eyes on the far end of the runway, I could see that I needed to press the right rudder right away, just to keep her running straight. I expected that. The speed began to build, and the tail lifted off the runway. My viewpoint, both from the cockpit and on flying in general, instantly changed. So did my centre line: I saw it begin to wander off to my right. I didn't expect *that*.

"Right rudder." Greer uttered the favourite words of a tailwheel flight instructor. I'd already pushed my right foot forward. We were running down the centre line again. The landscape on either side of the strip began to blur. The dewy grass and wild cotton struggling to survive along the runway's edges trembled in our wake. Far away, an engine roared, and the hiss of air caressing taut fabric replaced the trundling of rubber on runway.

Once we were in the air, the Citabria's lightness and responsiveness amazed me; its name is Airbatic spelled backwards. Being used to sloth-like high-wing trainers, I commented on how nicely it flew. Greer asked me to do a series of Dutch rolls — waggling the wings left and right — on the downwind leg of the circuit around the field.

I obliged, working hard with my hands and feet to keep the airplane's nose locked on a point on the horizon. I was either rock solid or all over the place. It was so hazy that I couldn't be sure I was actually rolling around a point at all. Holland Landing, shrouded in mist, slid by off my left shoulder.

Turning onto the final approach to land, the sheer drop of the cliff bordering the runway made me think that we might as well be landing on an aircraft carrier. Greer could probably do it in his sleep.

My airspeed control on the final approach was good. This Citabria didn't have flaps to help us descend and slow down, so I slipped, cocking the plane sideways to bleed off any excess altitude. As the speed dropped off to final approach numbers, I was feeling pretty good.

The edge of the cliff flashed by and away under the wings. The runway swam up. *Power off, stick back into the flare, and hold it here. Hold it. Be patient.*

A squeak, a slight hop, and we were down. A little shimmy of the nose as I found my feet again, then stick all the way back to pin the tail down.

That wasn't too bad, I thought to myself as we climbed for another go.

My next landing could have been an amusement park ride. I only remember the first bounce then bailing out of it with full power after what I'm sure was a minor stroke.

We flew a few less exciting circuits of the field, and we taxied clear of the runway. When we switched off and I climbed out, I saw my dad grinning from ear to ear.

"She almost caught you there, eh, son?"

"You could say that," I replied sheepishly.

"You know," he said, "in the Miniplane, sometimes it felt like you had to pedal her down the runway — like a bike. I had to move my feet that much. Otherwise, she'd bite you in the ass."

Aviation was, without a doubt, our strongest bond, and the one we spoke about the most. Flying was our church.

And yet, in a way, we were also strangers to each other. In the years he'd been working far from home, he'd missed watching me grow up. I had come to question the nomadic lifestyle he seemed to prefer. I convinced myself that my father worked out of town because construction projects in Ottawa just weren't interesting enough for a man of his skill and talent. That was true, but it wasn't the whole story: my dad didn't want to work those jobs because they were too close to home and offered too many reminders of his failed business. Simply put, my dad fled, and we lived with it because he seemed happy again. My dad was uncomfortable being static, and for this reason, I believe, he lived his life in a hurry. The next thing was always in the back of his mind, even when he had only just embarked on a new challenge. It could take a year, sometimes two, but eventually a once-stimulating project would become stale or a boss would begin to rub him the wrong way. He'd start working his way out — even if it meant self-sabotage.

It makes sense to me now. By the time my dad was in his mid-twenties, he had travelled the world. He married late. A family meant laying a foundation upon which to build a life. But putting down roots wasn't in Dad's nature. He loved us and was very proud of me and Vanessa, but in work he found a deep personal satisfaction, a purpose we couldn't give him.

The same summer that I earned my wings, Dad was diagnosed with melanoma, an aggressive cancer of the skin. He believed the disease stemmed from an injury a few years previous when he fell against a steel reinforcing bar and gashed his leg. But he had spent his entire professional career working outside on concrete slabs, baking in the sun. He used to brag that, even in his twenties, the formidable African mosquito would die trying to penetrate his leathery skin.

Whatever the cause, he had surgery to remove a tumour from his leg and tried to return to the construction site in Niagara. His boss threatened to fire him if he didn't take time to recover, so Dad propped himself up in bed with his laptop and worked from the motel room that served as his home. An apprentice delivered plans and schematics twice daily. His main motivation for getting better was to return to work.

By the time I found out about the diagnosis, the surgery had already taken place.

Eight

High above the lake, the faraway buzz of an airplane's engine is the only soundtrack to a breathtaking aerial ballet.

My dad's flying the airplane — a German-built aerobatic trainer called a Grob 115. Loop, hammerhead, another loop, and then a barrel roll. I'm watching him handle an airplane he's never flown before, doing manoeuvres he hasn't flown in thirty years. As we crest the top of the barrel roll, I watch his eyes flit from his pivot point to the nose then slide down the wing to the next reference. Hands and feet react to what his eyes see. He's had a rough time, my dad. The radiation treatments have beat him up pretty good. That's why we're up here, ballistic over the top of a loop now. He's earned this.

My dad is dying.

In 2007, the cancer returned. It's spread to his liver, stomach, and pancreas.

Yet here we are, gathering speed down the backside of the loop in silence, doing something we both love. We rush up the vertical line of another hammerhead. He hits it perfectly, leaning on the right rudder pedal with his ravaged leg, and sticks it there with just the right amount of forward stick. The Grob is ungainly, and we won't draw this line for too long. His good leg pushes his boot against the left rudder pedal. He's timed it flawlessly, which is critical.

The world stops. A sigh. Was it me? Him?

I can't tell.

The nose slices left as the rudder comes in to the stop. We're pointed straight at the centre of the earth again. I catch a glimpse of the

May sun shimmering on the lake's surface. Even into the spring, little flakes of ice have survived, huddled together in the middle of the lake. The sunlight leaks through the propeller's gossamer disc as the earth slides away beneath the belly.

"Okay, Pop," he says to me. "Let's go back. I'm done."

I knew this would be our final flight.

When it came to aviation, my father and I shared many traits, but one stood out from the rest: we bored easily. The ennui lay not in being aloft but in the type of airplane or the kind of flying it was engaged in. We obsessively sought new challenges. I followed a similar path to Dad's: after building enough flying experience, I qualified to fly at night and then earned a commercial licence that would permit me to fly for hire. Before the ink on my commercial licence was dry, I dove into aerobatics. Then I thought teaching others to loop and roll might be fun, and so I became a certified aerobatic flight instructor.

Once my youthful dream of flying for the military was dashed, I never planned to fly professionally. The climb to the captain's seat of a long-haul airliner, the pinnacle of commercial aviation, didn't appeal to me. I could expect to work long hours as an instructor, earning little pay and probably investing some of my own money in the pursuit of flight hours to get a job in the North or out West, flying a twin-engine airplane out of small communities. I could toil in the wilderness for years, jumping from job to job and outfit to outfit, until, if I was lucky, a regional carrier hired me. I might make it to one of the big airlines eventually, but two or three decades could pass before I'd finally be the captain, surveying the curvature of the earth from thirty-five thousand feet.

I liked sleeping in my own bed, despised moving, and even at a young age wanted to put down roots and have a family. I also worried that turning my passion into a career might grind the joy out of it.

I enjoyed writing. I went to university for journalism because I wasn't bright enough for engineering and feared getting out with an English degree wouldn't really be worth the cost of admission. My instructors were almost all battle-hardened veterans of the Fourth Estate. "Less is more," they growled. "One idea, one sentence. Subject and verb. Kill the rest." We agonized over each word, trimming here and there, simplifying without dumbing down, forging, hardening, tearing the soul out of it.

I discovered writing for radio. We were taught to write to the sound. Now, my neatly formed words — as effective as they could be in conveying an image, a smell, or a feeling — had a powerful ally in actual sound. I ended up in television journalism. I found it infinitely harder and more satisfying than writing for print. At times the story was so powerful that its characters and images did all the telling, and I hardly got a word in at all.

For nearly ten years, this was the sort of writing I toiled away at, first as a reporter and then as a show producer. My dad loved watching my reports on television. He saw a kinship in that we both worked at something and turned out a product after a period of time — something real and tangible. The switch to producing appealed to me because no longer would I be bound to a minute-and-a-half report. Rather, I'd be responsible for the whole show. Dad didn't get it and confessed he no longer understood what I did every day.

I once asked my dad why he had quit flying. We were on a short flight back to St. Catharines from Grimsby, where he had talked me through landing on a shockingly narrow ribbon of asphalt. I was nineteen, had just earned my wings, and couldn't understand why anyone would ever willingly give this up.

"Well, after your sister was born..." he began and then paused, his brow furrowed, and grimaced a little. He opened his mouth to continue, thought again, and shrugged. "I got cold feet," he eventually said.

"Cold feet?" It sounded like bullshit to me. "I don't know, Dad. I'll never give this up."

"Good," he replied gently. "I hope you never do. But one day you might understand why I did."

I thought about that a bit and then, with a little shrug, waved my hand at his control yoke.

"You want to fly it for a bit?"

He smiled, nodded slightly, and placed his right hand on the control column and his left on the throttle. He flew us back to St. Catharines as if no time had passed at all.

These were rare moments. While we flew together often, my dad only took the controls if I insisted. His reluctance had nothing to do with his lack of recent experience or confidence in his skill; in fact, his handling of the airplane in flight showed no ill effect from his decades away. His flying was effortless, flawless. Even on bumpy days, when the sky was so choppy that flying felt like riding twenty-foot swells in a dinghy, Dad seemed to will the airplane to fly smoothly. It was almost as if he could anticipate each jostle, when and from where it would come, and then guide the airplane through. Somehow, he managed to turn plunging precipices in the air currents into gentle ripples. One could sit next to him, pour a cup of coffee, and not spill a drop.

He left the flying to me because he saw it as a learning opportunity: he had logged many hours already, and I had very few to my name. He also refused to let me pay for any of the flights we took together. Each time we landed, he would go into the terminal ahead of me with the excuse of having to use the bathroom or grab something from the car. When it came time to settle the bill, he had already taken care of it. He called it an investment.

But Dad did a poor job of investing in himself, especially his health. He didn't get preventative checkups between his first and second diagnosis. He worked away from home, moved sites frequently, and did not have access to a regular doctor. The recurrence was far more severe. A team of doctors suggested a battery of treatments: chemotherapy, another surgery, radiation. It might get you another three to five years, they said. My dad did it all. Then the seizures started. I hurried out of a date with the woman who became my wife during one, and ducked out of a funeral an hour and a half out of town for another. I sat in a meeting with a doctor who looked worried about my dad's rapid weight loss. My dad patted his stomach and, with a wry smile, commented on how good he looked. The doctor started talking about symptom management, a nicer way to say end-of-life care.

Outwardly, my dad impressed visitors with his grace in the face of this terrible and indiscriminate killer. Privately, he was terrified, bitter, and angry. We all were. I imagine any family contending with a terminal illness has these same emotions as constant and malignant companions. My dad could say hurtful things. He didn't mean them. I know that now. But at the time, they were difficult to hear.

After one seizure he woke up while I was sitting at his hospital bedside. He took one look at me, said my name, and began to weep. I had never seen my dad cry.

"What is it, Dad?" I was tired and scared, and the words came out tersely.

"What did I do to you?" he asked. "Why are you mad at me?"

"I'm not mad," I lied. I was mad: at what cancer was doing to our family and at him, who, although resigned to his diagnosis and the inevitable result, seemed only to regret that he wasn't able to keep working. What angered me more than anything was what I felt he'd thrown away: a chance to grow older, know my wife, meet his grandchildren, play with them in the yard. And for what? To erect an interesting building in a city far from his family?

"What a fucking waste," I said to my mom that night.

I found out years later that Dad had told Vanessa: "I risked everything to work and travel the world, and look where I ended up."

One of the last times I saw him, he told me a Miniplane story.

"On the ground, she was such a *bitch*."

The words curled off his lips, dripping with contempt, with marked pauses between the last three. He let the last word hang in the air for effect. My dad was not one for dramatics.

"Uh huh," I replied. We were in the basement. A hockey game was on: the hometown Senators were in Toronto, losing to their bitter rivals, the Maple Leafs. I was only half watching. A Maple Leaf glided across the ice toward the Ottawa net and then, effortlessly, neatly slotted the puck through the goalkeeper's legs. The stadium erupted in jubilation. I winced, knowing Dad would hurl a barrage of insults at the television screen. He didn't understand the game, but he could read the scoreboard.

Silence. I looked across at him. My dad was crumpled on the couch, hands folded on his chest. It was warm in the house, but he'd lost so much weight he was always cold. That night, he was wearing a hat and coat. And he was smiling. Not at the screen, but at a point somewhere in the space beyond.

It had been twenty-five years since he'd last seen his biplane, but that's where he was: snug in the confines of the single cockpit, fighting to keep her on the runway at Rockcliffe while she protested her return to earth.

"Hey," I said, almost apologetically because I didn't want to ruin his reverie. "Why don't we look it up? It can't be that difficult to find."

"No." The response was terse but not unkind.

"Dad…"

"It's all right," he sighed, rising slowly from the couch. "I'm going to go for a walk."

I followed him upstairs. Jack, my beagle, padded along behind us. Dad went out. Jack hopped onto the couch in the living room, laid his head on the backrest, and watched him out the large front window. I walked down the hallway to my parents' bedroom, pulled open the drawer to the bedside table, and fished out my dad's logbook.

I turned it over in my hands. The soft, black suede slipcover, despite its age, looked and felt new. The button clasp opened with a snap. The logbook, too, was in good shape. My dad's addresses in Nairobi,

Termoli, and Toronto were listed inside the front cover. Flipping through the logbook felt almost voyeuristic. It is, after all, a very personal document, a chronicle of a pilot's flying life. The notations in my dad's precise hand were prosaic: date, aircraft type, registration, crew, time aloft, airport of origin and destination, and whatever comments he was moved to set down. Still, exotic place names rose from the pages: Magadi, Kajiado, Amboseli, Kakuzi, Keekorok, and Mombasa. The logbook afforded only an inch of space to write remarks. My dad's notes were mostly exercise numbers. If he'd performed aerobatics, however, he spelled out the manoeuvres in tight handwriting.

Some of the Canadian airports he visited no longer exist. Maple and King City have become, respectively, a subdivision and a construction yard. He misspelled some place names, notably Sudbury, Kapuskasing, and Parry Sound. He also recorded a scattering of flights into Toronto Pearson International Airport and the military base at Borden, back when they used to let you do that.

And finally, on the forty-fourth page, on June 11, 1981, began his record of his flights in the Smith. I ran my finger down the columns. The flights happened almost daily but they were short, rarely more than forty minutes with the average being less than a half hour. Next to a flight dated September 19, I found what I was looking for.

"Power-off approaches," my dad has written, "almost ground looped."

A gliding approach in the Smith is made at a blistering speed of one hundred miles per hour. The engine is at idle, and the extra speed helps slow the rate of descent as the aircraft is rounded out to a landing stance, or flared, just before touching down. At that speed, and without the invigorating blast of the propeller turning under power, things can go sideways in a hurry.

His words echoed in my head. That was the flight he was thinking about.

"Looking at the logbook?" Back from his walk, my dad stood in the doorway, watching me.

"Yeah. Look, Dad —"

"No," he interrupted with finality. "I don't want to know."

I closed the logbook and returned it to the bedside table drawer.

He passed away two days later, at age sixty-six, under the grey skies of a Thursday morning on February 9, 2012. I had been fighting the flu and had stayed away from my parents' home because Dad was weak and I was afraid of making him sick.

It was unusually warm for February, and the sound of rain spattering against the windowsill of the bedroom roused me from my sleep. I felt better but exhausted. The phone rang. My mother's voice was calm but weary, the voice of someone who had had enough of sickness and fear. She told me the doctor thought today might be the day that my dad would let go, but that we still had several hours.

Fifteen minutes later, I made the three-minute drive to my parents' house. The clouds were low, flat, and grey. The streets were quiet. When I walked through the front door, the doctor and my mother were standing in the living room. I knew before they could open their mouths. My dad was gone. I'd missed him by only a few minutes. I was twenty-eight, only a few months older than my father was when he lost his dad.

For a few long moments I just stood, not feeling anything. Then I went down the hall. I found Dad in my old bedroom. He looked strange, different than he had only two days before. I knew who he was, but I didn't recognize him. People had told me that, in death, their loved ones looked like they'd fallen asleep and could awake at any moment. Dad didn't look like that at all. His face was a mask. Not knowing what to do, and ashamed of the emptiness I felt, I bent down and kissed him on the forehead. I felt as though I was watching the scene play out from elsewhere in the room. I closed the door as I left, thinking, absurdly, that my father would prefer privacy.

Mom and Vanessa picked out a coffin made of cherrywood. I sorted through boxes and albums of photographs, arranged my choices chronologically, scanned them, and edited a video tribute to play in the funeral home during the visitations. I set the images to Iron & Wine's mournful "The Trapeze Swinger," and as the images rolled across my screen, I cried silently, afraid, in an empty house, that someone would hear me.

The visitations passed quickly; endless streams of people passed through, knelt by the coffin, stopped to watch the video. Some were friends of Vanessa's or mine who had never met our dad and had come to support us. But most had known him, and had a story or a fond memory. *How did this happen? He was so young. What a loss.* I nodded mechanically.

The next day, Vanessa and I gave the eulogy. I had prepared notes but didn't use them and don't remember what was said. Dad's casket sat in the aisle in front of a lit candle, a bunch of sunflowers, and a photograph of him standing in front of his biplane. Six of us — my cousins, my dad's cousin, two of his best friends, and I — carried the casket out the front doors of St. Anthony of Padua Church. It was still and cold. The bells tolling from the belfry sounded muffled, as if reluctant to shatter the peace. High above, an airliner laid out four razor-thin contrails across the blue sky, cleaving it neatly in half.

An hour later as we stood outside the rectangular vault, his death started to sink in. I held my mom's hand and put my arm around Vanessa's shoulders. The electric lift whined, labouring against the weight of the casket, lifting it up to the little space in the wall. It was a terrible, jarring sound. A granite stone was set in place and a hand drill screeched four times. Then a white piece of paper with my dad's name was taped to the centre. And that was it.

When I got home, I noticed the shoulder of my black suit had been stained beige by the makeup and tears of the family and friends who had embraced me over the last few days — powerful evidence of what my dad had meant to those he had known. I never wore that suit again.

Vanessa and I were both relieved. Finally, she felt, our years of fragmentation were over. Somehow, losing Dad made us whole again. I was glad his suffering was over. Now our family could focus on the future.

I thought things would get better. But when I thought about Dad, and I often did, I felt guilt for not being there at the end, for not having taken one more flight together, for not doing enough as a son. My regrets swelled and multiplied and kept me up at night.

They say not to make serious decisions after watershed events like the death of a loved one, but the summer after Dad died, Mom moved out of the house. She couldn't stay. The place was full of ghosts — phantoms she couldn't live with.

While packing up, she uncovered a nondescript manila envelope wedged under a banker's box stuffed with tax documents stored on the top shelf of the broom closet. Scrawled across the front of the envelope was a short note, written in pencil in my father's easily recognizable hand. "Jona — Please keep this envelope for me — this [is] the biplane logbook. Thanks Dad!"

The note made me laugh. Who signs off with an exclamation mark? The envelope contained full-sized photocopies of the pages of *FAM*'s logbook, but the entries only covered the time Charlie Miller owned the plane. After leafing through, I soon discovered why. Tucked in with the photocopies was a neatly folded piece of thin stationery — a letter from Charlie to my dad more than twenty-five years before, asking if he had sent the copy of the Smith's logbook. Clearly Dad never sent Charlie the photocopies (this was typical of my dad, but it was a product of inattention, not malice). A phone number for Charlie was written on the back of one of the pages. I tried calling him, but the number was, not surprisingly, no longer in service.

I decided to try to find *Foxtrot Alpha Mike*. I hoped that the search would, at the very least, give me something productive to do. It would free me from the carousel of regret I was feeling and help me reconnect with my father over our shared love of flight. I knew from my cursory online searches that *FAM*'s registration had lapsed in May 2000, so I was certain that she was no longer flying. It was possible, however, that somewhere the little biplane was hiding in the corner of an old barn or slowly sinking into the long grass of a neglected field. If I could find her, perhaps her owner might be persuaded to sell. There was a chance, however remote, that I could fly Dad's beloved Smith and return her to the skies.

Nine

Finding *Foxtrot Alpha Mike* turned out to be remarkably easy. My dad had sold her to a local pilot and mechanic, who in turn sold her to a bush pilot named Michel Lequin. Lequin was the designer of the Tapanee Levitation, a Canadian homebuilt bush plane. He'd owned and flown another Smith Miniplane before he bought *FAM*, one built by a man named Robert McLarnon in Atlantic Canada, likely Nova Scotia, in 1967. Lequin wrecked that Smith in the late eighties, prompting him to replace it with *FAM*. He disassembled her, loaded the pieces onto the back of a flatbed, and trucked them north to Sainte-Anne-du-Lac, a tiny hamlet about thirty miles north of Mont-Laurier, Quebec. He reassembled the pieces and made his first flight, a half-hour hop, two days later.

Lequin removed the original propeller and replaced it with a longer model. He intended to use the biplane for aerobatics, but he considered the engine underpowered. While he searched for a better engine, he put in nearly thirty hours flying short, local trips.

By April 1991, *FAM* was eighteen years old and needed more work. Her top wing showed some twisting, and Lequin decided to rebuild it. He moved the airplane into a friend's hangar. Having found an engine, he removed the faithful Continental that had carried the plane through roughly one thousand hours and in and out of airports from Maple, Ontario, to Sainte-Anne-du-Lac, Quebec. With the engine removed, *FAM* weighed less than five hundred pounds. Before Lequin could install the replacement, a summer storm ripped through the airport. His friend had moved the Smith outside so he could work on his own plane, and although he called Lequin to warn him that the storm was coming, Lequin didn't make it to the airport in time to tie the Smith down. The wind picked *FAM* up and flung her thirty feet across the ramp. She landed on her back, her tail's vertical stabilizer crushed and the rebuilt top wing crumpled.

His work ruined, Lequin didn't think it made financial sense to repair the airplane. He pushed the biplane behind the hangar and left her — her sides laid open, her wings limp, and her button nose discarded on the grass under the cavity that once held her engine. For nine years, clouds slipped overhead slowly in the sky she used to dance in. Her cherry-red paint began to wear away, exposing patches of the original blue. With every passing gust of wind, her frame creaked and groaned.

In 2000, local pilot Alain Maille happened by. For as long as Maille could remember, he had wanted to fly a biplane. Her wings were damaged, her trail crushed. She had no engine and no instruments and was missing various other parts, pieces, and fabric. But Maille saw only promise.

Maille bought the Smith for $5,000 and trucked it south to his home in Mont-Laurier. Maille kept her in his garage for five years. He loved the biplane and always believed he would restore it to flying condition. Yes, she needed work, but her structure was sound. He nurtured the dream until his second plane needed some restoration work. It broke his heart, but he sold the Smith to a firm that built play structures and decorations for parks and zoos, making back his original investment.

Before the Smith was trucked off yet again, Maille, for reasons he fails to recall, removed the aircraft's data plate — legally, the essence of the airplane. One could, in theory, rebuild a Smith Miniplane around the data plate, and it would, in legal terms, be *Foxtrot Alpha Mike*. He tucked the data plate into the back pouch of the Smith's journey log. When I spoke to Maille and explained the purpose of my inquiries, Maille sent me both the journey log and the data plate.

By the time Alain Maille found Foxtrot Alpha Mike *at*
Sainte-Anne-du Lac, the plane had seen better days.
(Photograph courtesy Alain Maille)

Less than a week later, I held *Foxtrot Alpha Mike*'s journey log in
my hands. An aircraft's journey log is its life story. *FAM*'s is lovely. It's
enveloped in a well-worn, forest-green cover with the Canadian coat
of arms and the words *Department of Transport* embossed in fading
gold. A strip of red ticker tape bears the airplane's registration, but the
colour has long since worn away. You have to tilt the book to catch the
light to read the lettering. The log has the comforting, musty smell of
a favourite library book. On its pages, every detail, flight by flight, is
recorded: maintenance notes, modifications, and, if the pilot so chose,
observations or events. As I ran my finger down the columns of entries
by Muller, Miller, Rotondo, and Lequin, *FAM*'s life — nearly a thousand hours in the air — leapt off the yellowing pages. I poured a scotch,
and followed the entries to the very end. This was the story of a plane
that introduced a little boy to the magic and wonder of flight.

I found the data plate in a clear plastic envelope taped to the inside of the back cover. The envelope also contained old documents, like government airworthiness certificates, maintenance forms, and notices. The data plate was only slightly larger than a razor blade. Crudely engraved on one side, it read:

REG. CF-FAM
SMITH-MINI-PLANE
SERIAL NO EM 8936
BUILT SEPT. 10, 1973
ERNST MULLER REXDALE

Foxtrot Alpha Mike's *data plate.*

I turned the data plate over in my hand to find that someone had used a file to remove previous markings and stamp new ones in their place. I ran my fingers over the roughly engraved lettering.

SMITH DSA-1
REG. CF-FAM
SERIAL – 8730
1971
FRED A. MCGREGOR

Hot pangs of guilt burned deep inside my chest. If only I had done this even a year earlier, when Dad was still alive. I needed a way to process this pain, or at least a place I could put it. And so I began blogging, chronicling my dad's flying life and how he came to fly *Foxtrot Alpha Mike*. But I wanted to do more.

Maille had told me that I would find my dad's biplane in the Granby Zoo, south of Montreal. An image search turned up some pictures. The airplane in the grainy photographs looked nothing like the craft I remembered. It was certainly a Smith but had more of a hunchback shape. The colours, too, were wrong: canary yellow slashed in white and blue instead of cherry red and white. Then I used an online mapping tool to navigate through the zoo and discovered that her paint scheme had been changed to orange and blue. I contacted the zoo, explained the plane's significance to me, and asked if it would consider selling her. The zoo was not interested in selling. It had recently covered the biplane in $15,000-worth of fibreglass — roughly what a Smith in flying condition might fetch. The only salvageable part might have been the fuselage — and even that was a long shot.

I had thought I would be excited to go and see it, but I wasn't. I just didn't feel ready to face this part of my past so soon after my father's death. The guilt I felt for not insisting on tracking *FAM* down while my dad was still alive only deepened with how easily I had found her. Worse, the closure I expected to find never materialized. I still felt empty.

But then I thought back to one of my favourite movies when I was a kid — a Disney made-for-TV film titled *The Blue Yonder*. I had watched it so many times that I wore the tape out. It tells the story of an eleven-year-old boy, also named Jonathan, who uses a time machine to travel back to the 1920s and stop his grandfather from making a fatal solo attempt to fly across the Atlantic. Halfway through the film is a scene where Jonathan sees his grandfather's biplane for the first time. The hangar doors are pushed open and the light spills in. A beautiful biplane emerges slowly from the shadows, the light reflecting off its polished-chrome propeller hub, dancing across her pale-blue flanks and along the flying wires. How magical it would have been to have someone pull off a dusty old tarp to reveal my dad's airplane — in rough shape, perhaps, but intact and needing only time, patience, and money to fly again. I comforted myself with the knowledge that Dad's Smith still existed, that children were playing on her, and the seeds of future pilots were being sown on that playground.

Rather than see the airplane in her current state, I kept writing, researching, and making connections with people from my dad's past. One of the first people I contacted was Murray Sinton, my dad's first instructor. I found a man with that name and of roughly the right age through Facebook, and I sent him a note asking if he'd taught at Wilken Aviation in the 1970s. My shot in the dark found its mark. More than four decades later and happily retired from a long aviation career, Sinton remembers my dad as a diligent and enthusiastic student who had the natural ability and judgment needed to fly. Sinton left the Wilken school after two years to fly for a charter company in Kenya. He ended his career as a corporate pilot in South Africa, flying the Canadian-designed Challenger series of business jets. He still has in his possession the small silver eagle, the emblem of civilian pilots in Italy, my father gave him when he received his wings. (Years later, Dad and I commissioned several more from a Niagara jeweller; I gave one to Nigel Barber, my instructor at Les Cèdres.) From Sinton I learned that Clive Corner is retired and living in the UK. Mike Amos, the instructor who would rap students on their knees whenever they made a mistake, passed away a few years ago, and the chief pilot Alan Coulson may also be gone. Paul Lennox's story is the most tragic of the lot. While piloting a charter flight in Uganda in May 1978, his plane exploded, killing everyone on board. One of his passengers, Kenyan politician Bruce McKenzie, had inadvertently brought on board a bomb disguised as a gift from the dictator Idi Amin.

The next man I contacted, again through internet searches, was Lee Heitman. Heitman continued Dad's aerobatic training after he arrived in Canada, picking up where Biff had left off. Dad remembered that Heitman wore cowboy boots when he flew and piloted with such precision that he could eight-point roll a little Cessna 150 Aerobat, stopping the aircraft crisply at every 45 degrees of roll — no easy feat. Heitman remembers that Dad was a natural aerobatic pilot and very enthusiastic about the sport and life in general.

A portrait of a man began to come into focus, one quite different from the person I knew. The man these people had known, however briefly, seemed free. He had less on his mind. He didn't worry about money. If he had problems, he handled them better, or at least seemed to. These were days when he ran *to* things rather than away from them. I shared my impressions with Mom. She said that before the business failed, Dad was a lot of fun. I don't remember much from those years, and what I do are mere fragments of memories: Dad, in an overcoat and loafers, beating me in a foot race; or the time he broke his glasses on a hike and laughed as he threw them down the wooded hillside. Old photos provided more evidence: there he was cuddling on the couch with me as a baby, flashing a lopsided grin from the cockpit of *FAM*, and hamming it up in a floppy hat, fur coat, and leather driving gloves. He *was* different in our first years together. Ultimately, there weren't enough of those years for us to enjoy.

I put what I'd learned of *FAM*'s story to paper for a three-part series the Canadian Owners and Pilots Association published in its newspaper in 2014. These articles generated a good number of notes, emails, and phone conversations with people who had more pieces to the puzzle.

I really wanted to talk to Charlie Miller and had made an honest effort to track him down. Ernie Muller was unable to provide contact information, internet searches failed, and calling all the Charles Millers, Charlie Millers, and C. Millers in Ontario would have required a robot dialer. Miller's trail had gone cold — and then, out of the blue, an email from him landed in my inbox. He'd read the articles I'd published and decided to get in touch with me. I sent him the logbook copies my dad had promised to him all those years ago,

AEROBATICS CANADA - CHAPTER 3. 12 NOVEMBER 1989

Len	Gerry	Ben	Carole	Bohdan	Larry	Patricia	Larry & Elaine	Charlie
Goodman	Younger	Ciantar	Holyk	Shrynk	Weeks	Cruchley	Ernewein	Miller

	Lorie	Kerry	Biff
	Jocius	Cornelius	Hamilton

Aviation, particularly aerobatics, is a very small world.
This Aerobatics Canada — Chapter Three photo includes Gerry Younger,
who prepared my dad to fly his Smith, Charlie Miller, and Biff Hamilton.
(Photograph courtesy of Charlie Miller)

filling a gap in his own flying history. He reciprocated with reams of photographs and a magazine article featuring *FAM* at Brampton.

Charlie's vivid recollections of his time flying the Smith gave me a new idea. I knew *FAM* would never fly again; I wasn't going to be able to recreate my dad's experience that way. But I could fly a Smith of my own.

I briefly considered building one around *FAM*'s data plate — or rather, having one built for me, since I didn't have the skills to do it myself. That would require a team of people working over several years and cost mountains of money before I could roll a new *FAM* out of the hangar. It was a tantalizing but unattainable dream.

Since I had the data plate, I considered buying a Smith Miniplane and reregistering it with *FAM*'s old marks. There was, however, one major hurdle: the plane was never properly deregistered. Her registration marks remained attached to her hulk, and she remained on Transport Canada's books. Deregistration meant sending Transport Canada letters from *FAM*'s last owner and the person who had custody of the wreck. A letter from the zoo assuring Transport Canada that the airplane would never fly again was easy enough to obtain. But Maille's purchase of *FAM* was never properly reported or recorded. He was the last owner of the airplane but, as far as Transport Canada was concerned, Lequin was the last *registered* owner. Lequin, who had no idea what had happened to the plane after Maille trucked it away, could not provide a letter. When I volunteered that I had the Smith's data plate, Transport Canada asked that I return it immediately to ensure it couldn't be improperly attached to another plane. I asked what they intended to do with it and was told it would be destroyed. I hung up the phone. When I held the data plate in my hand, I held my dad's biplane. I wasn't going to give that up.

I decided the data plate would never be applied to another plane: there would only be one *Foxtrot Alpha Mike*. Instead, I would find a Canadian-built Smith and, guided by my father's legacy, chart my own course.

ALOFT, ALOW

Ten

My dad had died in February, and the flying season began in late March. I was looking forward to getting back to instructing on the weekends. But when I showed up for a weekend shift on the first Saturday of April, I realized that my instructor rating had expired. I was no longer able to teach.

I decided to upgrade my instructor rating to the senior level, which would allow me to train new aerobatic instructors. I asked Andrew Campbell, who had trained me for my initial rating, for help. By July, I was qualified to teach again, and while I enjoyed it, I couldn't shake my sorrow. My dad had been a constant in my flying activities. He was the first person I called after I soloed for the first time. He was waiting for me on the ground after my first aerobatics and tailwheel lessons. He was the first to find out I'd earned my commercial license and an aerobatic instructor rating. I wanted to share this milestone with him too.

The idea of buying a Miniplane burrowed deeper into my mind and began to gnaw at me. As I prepared for my senior instructor rating, I browsed the internet for Smiths that were on the market. They were all US-based, and most were unfinished projects that would require time and more money than I had. People who had bought planes advised me to look in Canada. I went through the public files on each Smith in the government's registry and emailed or called the most promising hits. Did they still have their Smith? Would they be interested in selling? Time and time again, the answer was no. The closest I got to a Smith was one that was being rebuilt near Gananoque, about two hours southwest of Ottawa. The owner admitted he'd be open to selling, but it would take a few years of work before it would fly again.

Now it was November, and I was still searching.

On a brisk, early November morning, a thick blanket of fog lay close to the ground at Rockcliffe, blotting out the sunshine. Overhead and unseen, I could hear the clattering roar of a 1940s WACO open-cockpit biplane circling the field. The pilot was waiting for the fog to burn away so that he could begin his day of hopping tours of the capital and the Gatineau Hills, where the fall's spectacular mosaic of colours still remained. The windsock hung limply from its bracket over the fuel pumps.

"So you're looking for a Miniplane?" asked Ed Soye, an old friend from my cadet days. He had his hands in his pockets and his face turned upward to the murky skies. He tracked the noise of the WACO's radial engine as it waned and grew, depending on where it was in its orbit of the field. It was a distinctive sound — *pock, pock, pock* — and you could hear each of the seven cylinders as they fired, driving its big wooden propeller around into a blur. Ed was a well-regarded vintage airplane display pilot and looked the part. Professionally, he was an equity analyst for a large firm in Toronto, but he looked like he should be wearing goggles and a helmet in the cockpit of a Second World War fighter. (In fact, Ed has recently left the boardroom and joined the RCAF as a pilot.)

"Yep," I said, kicking at the ramp.

"Well, why didn't you say so?"

I looked up, raising an eyebrow.

The bracket mounted to the airport fuel tank creaked, and the windsock stirred. A breath of wind drifted across the field from the southwest. Soon, the breeze would break apart the fog, and the WACO would thread its way down through the mist and lower itself soundlessly onto Rockcliffe's single runway. Ed and I headed into the clubhouse.

Ed's first experience flying warbirds was piloting replica First World War airplanes with the Great War Flying Museum at the Brampton airport. One of the other pilots had built a couple of airplanes, including a Smith. Ed told me it was kept in flying condition, but the owner was so busy flying another plane he'd built and flying for the museum that he rarely had time to fly the Smith. He thought the owner might be willing to sell it and offered to put us in touch if I was interested. If?

A few emails, a phone call, and four months later, I slowly lowered myself into the tight confines of a Smith Miniplane's cockpit carefully placed in the corner of a heated hangar at the Brampton airport, just outside Toronto. This Smith was white with red trim, a red cowling, and a black cheat line that stretched from nose to tail along each side. The tops of the wings held a fine layer of dust, and the paint was worn in a few places around the tail, but visually, at least, the little biplane was in great shape.

Al Girdvainis, her builder and only owner, stood next to me, telling me about his plane. His left foot was on the wing walk, his left hand draped casually over the top wing. As he spoke, he drummed his fingers on the taut fabric. I couldn't shake the feeling that I could hear my dad's voice too.

Al was in high school in the mid-sixties when he first decided to build an airplane. He had his heart set on another type, a low-wing monoplane speed demon known as the Midget Mustang. Then he saw the Smith Miniplane and caught the biplane bug in the worst possible way. After he came across a local Miniplane (the one owned by local EAA president George Jones), his jaw dropped. There was just something about it. With several Miniplanes flying locally, and a wealth of knowledge and experience nearby, it seemed the obvious choice. He ordered the plans from Dorothy Smith, Frank's widow.

He spent years building the wings in his parents' basement. His dad didn't own a metal band saw, so he used a hacksaw and file to hand-cut the metal fittings for the wings and fuselage. Another Miniplane pilot introduced him to a de Havilland welder who built the Smith's steel fuselage. Al would drive to Downsview Airport with steel tubing, and this guy would weld the pieces together for him. Al is tall, so he had the welder add six inches to the length of the fuselage to make the cockpit roomier. One day, Al returned to the house with a complete fuselage, which he kept in the garage.

Al added another six inches of wingspan on either side of the centre-line to, he joked, improve glide performance. When the wings were finally ready, his dad helped him carefully slide them through the small basement windows. He then hung a 115 horsepower Lycoming engine on the front end — plenty of power for a small biplane. By August 1979, his project was complete.

The airplane was a joy to fly, but she could be nasty on the ground, especially on pavement, Al told me. "I've landed this thing without even touching the rudder pedals," he said. "And I've landed it by dancing a polka, double-time. I'm not trying to scare you. I just want you to know what you might be getting yourself into."

I visited with Al and his Smith for about an hour. This is his first airplane, and although he has since built an immaculate Vans RV-7A from a kit and was working on a replica of a First World War Nieuport 28 biplane, the Smith clearly held a special place in his heart. But I wouldn't be a position to make an offer for at least another year. I'd recently become engaged and had a wedding to plan. I hoped to fit in purchasing a biplane somewhere between the wedding and starting a family. I climbed out of his biplane and asked Al to give me a call if anyone came around asking about it. He agreed.

I had met Melody in October 2011. Like my parents, we were fixed up by friends. She had a background in dance and drama but opted for an education degree rather than life as a performer. She taught dance and religion at a local Catholic high school. We met on a football field behind a high school. She had just finished a charity run with a friend. I had spent the last two hours playing flag football and was slathered in mud. She went out with me anyway. She loved running, travel, and extreme roller coasters. That she'd tried bungee jumping and skydiving told me she had the necessary spirit for aerobatics.

A little more than a year after we first met, I proposed. I wanted to do something unexpected and unique with a touch of drama.

On a foggy evening, Melody met me at Rockcliffe for one last short flight before the end of the season. We took off and climbed: I was in the single seat in the front with Melody behind me. Melody's father, sister, and best friend, along with my mom and sister, hurried out to the side of the runway, holding signs that, when read in sequence, asked her to marry me. As we swung around for a low pass, I asked Melody to look out the left side and check the runway for ice. She gasped as we swept past the signs. I reached over my shoulder and handed her the ring.

Melody and I soon settled on a venue for our wedding — a restaurant in a building my dad had built on the shore of Ottawa's Mooney's Bay — but there were only two available dates, one in May and one in October. Given it was already March, I pushed heavily for October. Melody, confident in her planning skills, wanted May. After some discussion, she relented. "Patience is a virtue," she said, unwittingly uttering a phrase my dad often used.

My knees buckled. I sat down and wept. This common phrase took on an overwhelmingly emotional meaning for me. *How like him*, I thought, *to make his presence known on an occasion like this, in a place he'd built.* It was a connection I desperately needed.

☉

I'd been flying for twelve years and accumulated roughly six hundred and fifty hours in some twenty different types of planes. This wasn't a tremendous amount of experience by any means, but it was varied, and I'd picked up many transferable skills. For one, about half of my total flying experience had been in taildraggers, most of that in the back seat of the Super Decathlon. I was comfortable being blind out the front and using peripheral vision to land the airplane. The Super Decathlon, however, is forgiving and benign; it's a nice airplane for tailwheel neophytes to learn on.

I set out to find some relevant dual instruction that would prepare me for the shifty Smith Miniplane. More than thirty years before, my dad went to see Gerry Younger at Kitchener-Waterloo and logged about two hours in a Pitts S-2A. I found Andrew Boyd, a Pitts Special guru, aerobatic instructor, and air show pilot, at the Smiths Falls airport, a little less than an hour southwest of my home in Ottawa.

In the time it took me to drive down the taxiway between the rows of hangars, two airplanes rolled by. Boyd, standing outside his hangar, chatting with a fellow pilot, acknowledged each one with a wave. He was wearing a United States Navy–style leather aviator's jacket, track pants, and indoor soccer shoes. A pair of rose-coloured sunglasses were topped off by inquisitive eyebrows. He casually directed me where to park, and I climbed out of the car.

The front bumper of my car was splintered and hanging loosely in one spot, the result of an unfortunate meeting with a snowbank the winter before. Boyd studied it with keen interest. "You know," he said, "I just might have something for that." He disappeared inside the hangar before emerging with a hand drill and a bag of zip ties.

A stiff crosswind blew across the field. It would be a good day for my first flight in the immortal Pitts Special, but this was an odd start.

"Do you mind?" he asked.

"By all means," I laughed. "It can't get any worse."

Somewhat gleefully, Boyd drilled holes in my bumper. Every so often, he strung a zip tie through an opening and yanked it tight, and then clipped off the end with a pair of wire cutters. In a few minutes, he stepped back and admired his work. I gave the bumper a good shake. It held.

"If it were a black car, you'd hardly notice," he said, grinning as he offered an outstretched hand. "I'm Andrew."

"Jonathan."

"Hi! Let's get started."

For the Boyds, flying was the family business. Three generations flew formation aerobatics together, and three Pitts S-2Bs and a Maule M-4, a family heirloom, sat in the hangar. The floor was immaculate, and so were the airplanes. A trio of motorcycles was lined up in a far corner. The back of the hangar contained a workshop and a small apartment. Andrew had set up a makeshift classroom in the corner nearest the door, complete with two lawn chairs, a small whiteboard, and a model of an S-2. A dachshund padded across the back of the hangar, his belly barely clearing the gleaming floor. He lived there too.

Andrew's brain moved swiftly, and at first mine struggled to keep up. But he was a patient and generous teacher. As the ground-based preamble to flight concluded, I found myself catching my breath at the realization that the flying part of this adventure was going to be a thousand times more enjoyable, educational, and taxing.

Our mount for the day was the Pitts S-2B N666VB. The triple-six American registration and the fact that the airplane had been rebuilt after a fatal crash two decades previous only added to the red-and-white plane's devilish appearance. The words *Pale Horse* were painted under the canopy rim, a not-so-subtle nod to the Four Horsemen of the Apocalypse.

Andrew said the first time he flew the Pitts, it tried to kill him. The stick jammed during a vertical downline which, in Andrew's words, made for a very interesting landing. He felt compelled to buy it anyway.

About twenty minutes later, my left hand moved forward as the Pitts's engine went from a low, Harley Davidson-like rumble to a full-throated roar—260 pale horses pushed me back in my seat. Completely blind out the front, I paid particular attention to the pavement I could see out each side. I pushed the stick forward to raise the tail. The airplane responded sweetly and without delay. The tail came up, and I could now see down the length of the runway. The airplane quivered around me, longing for flight and buoyed by the increasing speed of the air rushing over the wings and the insistent battle cry of its engine.

A gentle tug, and we were off and climbing at a blistering rate. Andrew directed me to the south of the field where we'd spend some time doing aerobatics. The goal was to feel more comfortable before bringing the plane back to the airport to practise takeoffs and landings. After some acceptable rolls, loops, Cuban eights, spins, and inverted flying, Andrew and I returned to the circuit at Smiths Falls.

My first approach and landing in the Pitts went well. I concentrated on keeping my movements small and deliberate and knowing exactly where I was throughout. I stayed light on my feet, and only went to full power for the takeoff once I was sure I had her under control. After a half-dozen circuits, I started to get tired. Everything happened fast in the Pitts, and it took most of my awareness and skill just to keep up. Andrew offered me several tips and techniques, and we agreed to do a few more sessions.

The Pitts left me tingling and light-headed, and I drove home in a bit of a haze. Still, I felt good about the flying and was confident it would prepare me for the Smith. My car's firmly attached front bumper was an unexpected bonus.

I flew two more flights in the Pitts with Andrew. Each trip felt like the equivalent of cramming a master's degree into one sleep-starved week. Through it all, Andrew was brutally honest in his critique but incredibly generous when I did something well. After a little more than three hours, I felt good enough to move on to the Smith.

Fourteen months after first laying eyes on Al Girdvainis's Smith, I was newly married, I had saved and borrowed (but not stolen) $13,500, and was ready to take the plunge. I was back at the hangar in Brampton, waiting for my friend Pat Giunta, an aviation mechanic, to give Smith Miniplane *Charlie Golf Delta Sierra Alpha*, or *DSA*, a complete pre-buy inspection.

Coming up with enough money to buy an airplane isn't the hard part. It's the funds needed to maintain it that can trip up new owners. Everything costs money: space in a hangar or an outside tie-down to park the plane in, insurance, fuel, and oil. During the flying season, costs amount to about $400 a month and drop to roughly half of that during the winter when the Smith sits in storage. I made sure I wasn't getting in over my head by spending most of the year before buying the airplane budgeting as if I already owned it.

Al and I had spent most of the day going through the plane. He'd removed the cowling, the side and belly panels, the turtle deck, and the many inspection plates. With the biplane's steel bones laid bare and wiring exposed like muscle and sinew, it hardly looked like an airplane at all. Coffee in hand, we talked Miniplanes as we went through his, piece by piece. I asked Al about the airplane's serial number — the same as my birth year — and he told me he chose it because it was already stamped on a bit of steel tubing the de Havilland welder chose for the engine mount.

Although the Smith is a homebuilt that I am legally allowed to maintain myself, I decided to seek the help of an aviation maintenance engineer. I've never been a technically inclined person. I have a good understanding of the aircraft I fly and its systems, but I leave the wrenching to those who know what they are doing. Anything I am able to do will be done under their guidance. Still, I valued the opportunity to learn the inner workings of the airplane I hoped to buy and fly.

Talk inevitably turned to the more than thirty years and nearly six hundred hours Al spent flying *DSA*. An easy but slight smile crossed his face as he told me about two trips to Oshkosh, Wisconsin, the Mecca of experimental and homebuilt aviation, and a pair of voyages out east. He laughed nervously as he recounted crossing the Northumberland Strait from New Brunswick to Prince Edward Island by following the nearly thirteen-kilometre-long Confederation Bridge; the Smith's tail barely cleared the thick layer of cloud above. On another trip, Al and a friend followed a set of power lines carved

*Pat Giunta (left) joins Al Girdvainis as he runs up the Smith's
engine during our pre-buy inspection.*

through more than three hundred kilometres of wilderness with only
a single stop for fuel. These trips took guts, and it was clear that Al
enjoyed every second.

Pat arrived and started looking the plane over, sticking his head
inside *DSA*'s fuselage, peering into the wings with a flashlight. He
worked slowly and at first didn't say much. I'd been waiting for this
day for months with, I'll admit, a great deal of trepidation. I'd told
myself that I'd walk away if Pat found anything that indicated a
looming problem. It would break my heart, but I'd do it just the same.
Certain items — corrosion in the engine or airframe and rot in the
wings — were instant deal breakers.

I watched Pat closely. At first, his gaze was hard and focussed,
betraying little information and absolutely no emotion. Occasionally,
he took a step back to snap a picture. After what seemed like an eternity, only as he began inspecting the inner workings of the left wing
did he appear to relax a little bit. He muttered softly to himself as he

hunched under the upper wing, craning his neck as he tried to man-oeuvre the beam of his flashlight into the darkest corners. Finally, he nodded his approval and complimented Al on the condition of his Smith.

"Okay, that'll do it," he said. He wiped his hands on his trousers. "Let's push her out and fire her up."

We manoeuvered the little biplane onto a patch of grass outside the hangar doors, and Al hopped in. As he went through the pre-start checks, Pat and I stood in the shade of the hangar, arms crossed, watching. "This will tell us a lot," Pat said to me. I could hear my heart thumping in my head. Al hadn't started the engine in almost three years.

The prop swung, whipping around twice before the Lycoming burst to life and settled into an even purr. Al, silver hair blowing in the wind, grinned widely — but not at us. He was peering around the squared-off windshield, letting the propeller blast play across his face. He was firmly anchored on the ground but lost in the exuberance of flight, reliving some of the moments he'd spent in this plane.

Pat hollered his approval over the sound of the engine, slapped me on the back, and walked out to join Al. He peered over the side of the cockpit at the instrument panel. Both men pointed, nodded, and smiled. My anxiety began to melt away. It was starting to look like this might happen after all. A little more than an hour later, after checking the engine following the run-up, Pat and I pored over the pages of *DSA*'s weathered logbooks as we waited for lunch in the airport restaurant.

DSA's first flight took place on August 3, 1979, but Al wasn't at the controls. He asked an experienced pilot named Nick Daniel to take the Smith up for its inaugural flight and a few hours of testing and troubleshooting. Daniel was a former member of the Rothmans Aerobatic Team, Britain's first full-time civilian aerobatic team (in contrast to the Snowbirds, Blue Angels, and Thunderbirds, which are military teams). The Rothmans pilots, all highly trained former military men, thrilled crowds across Europe and Asia in the 1970s, first in Belgian Stampes and later American Pitts biplanes. Another member of the team was Neil Williams, the Calgary-born giant of aviation and talented author. His *Aerobatics* remains one of the most influential books about aviation ever written; my dad's copy, missing its dust jacket but complete with my toddler doodles, is on my bookshelf. Daniel was the team's commentator, spare pilot, and de facto manager. He and Al first crossed paths when Al was working as an air traffic controller at Toronto's Buttonville Airport. Daniel's hours of flying high-performance, squirrelly biplanes made him the perfect test pilot for the Smith.

Over a three-week period, Daniel flew a total of seven flights and kept meticulous notes that, despite being written nearly forty years ago, appear to have been set down only yesterday. Seven sheets of notes survive in the Smith's technical records, one for each flight. They tell the story of a pilot tentatively feeling out a new ship. The goal of his first flight was simply to ensure that the Smith was airworthy: that it was capable of stable flight and wouldn't fall apart around him. He wore a parachute, just in case. As the airplane passed each test and he grew more comfortable, he progressively explored the limits of the controls, flying it faster and higher. He moved on to stalls, spins, and, on his fourth flight, a roll. He noted that the airplane tended to hop during takeoffs from rougher grass fields and that it might be possible to become airborne before the biplane (or pilot) was ready and even to strike the propeller against the ground. He worked out the stall, approach, and gliding speeds, mostly through trial and error, and ensured that the instrumentation didn't lie too badly before pronouncing *DSA* fit for service.

Al made his first flight four days later and, from that day until 2007, he flew the Smith almost daily from April until November. Many flights were business — trips from a small grass field near his home to work at Buttonville. Others, like Charlie's, were purely for fun: local romps, flights into nearby grass fields for fly-in breakfasts, formation flying, and longer cross-country adventures. Together, Al and the Smith covered the eastern half of Canada and parts of the northern United States. Then, in 2007, Al and a friend finished building their Van's RV-7A. They could make longer trips in less time and in greater comfort; plus, the RV had an extra seat. Solo trips in the Smith lost their allure. Except for two quick hops in 2011, she sat in her corner of the hangar, well-maintained but not used.

Low-time, older airplanes are not desirable in the same way a low-mileage car is. Airplanes need to fly, or they rust and rot. The best way to keep an airplane healthy is to turn money into fuel and fuel into flight. Despite the period of inactivity, Pat's inspection revealed no red flags. He snapped the logbook closed. "Looks like you're buying this airplane," he said just as our burgers arrived.

On Tuesday, June 17, 2014, we made the purchase official. I spent the following day rolling my Smith up and down the runways, just as Al, Charlie, and my dad once did. Soon, I was doing faster runs.

By Thursday afternoon, I was convinced I was ready to practise taxiing with the tail in the air, as it would be in the moments before takeoff when the airplane gathers the speed necessary for flight. I had tentatively explored how much power and forward stick I would need to get the tail to fly, but had run out of runway and nerve before having any success. According to Al, I needed at least 2,000 rpm out of the engine along with nearly full-forward stick. Now, with Al's words echoing in my ears, I lined up on Brampton's ribbon-like runway and goaded the biplane on with power. I was growing comfortable taxiing the airplane in the three-point attitude to about fifty miles per hour. I could keep her going straight by tapping the rudder pedals to move the tailwheel and thus maintain the desired direction. The biplane's nose stayed obediently in line with the asphalt ahead, give or take a few degrees.

As the noise grew and our speed built, I felt the little biplane tremble around me. Not wanting to tear my eyes from the edges of the runway framing the plane's long nose, I stole a furtive glance at the tachometer. Its needle quivered at the 2,000 rpm mark. Without thinking, I pushed the stick forward into the darkness beneath the instrument panel. Suddenly and, frankly, before I was ready for it, the tail came up and the nose came down. The runway lay ahead. I was shocked. I'd been running the Smith up and down these strips for three days, but this was the first time I could look down their entire length. With the tail up, the view was breathtaking. The runway ran straight for what looked like forever, flanked on either side by my plane's red cabane struts and seemingly balanced on her chrome spinner. I'd launched hundreds of flights from dozens of strips like this one. But this was different.

It was exactly what you'd expect to see right before takeoff in a taildragger, but it came too quickly. A wave of ice-cold fear froze the euphoria. As swiftly and violently as a hammer striking a pane of glass, my confidence shattered.

No, no, no, no, no! my mind shrieked. *I'm not ready!*

I panicked. I cut the throttle to idle with my left hand, sharply, violently. Robbed of the rush of speed and blast of air from the propeller, my little plane heeled right. I pulled the stick back and dropped the tailwheel to the ground, making matters worse. The biplane's swerve increased. We were pointing toward the right edge of the runway — perhaps twenty-five feet and a split second away.

I'd only just bought the airplane — this steel, wood, and fabric embodiment of my childhood dream — and now I was going to wreck it. I thought to move my left foot hard against the rudder, but it was already there. Slowly, with painful indolence, the biplane began to turn left and away from disaster. I looked over the side of the cockpit rim and watched as the right wheel just barely kissed the edge of the pavement. The plane spun around slowly and finished pointing in the direction from which we'd come.

My ears were ringing behind the deafening beat of my heart. *How could I do something so stupid?* I was shaking. Not a subtle trembling of the hands, but a violent quaking. My teeth chattered uncontrollably. I was still on an active runway and needed to clear the strip. Somehow, I taxied back to Al's hangar and shut down in the shade of the open door. The hangar was deserted. Al was probably getting some lunch. I tried to pull myself out of the cockpit, but I couldn't feel my legs. So I sat and listened to the ticking of the engine cooling down. At some point, my heart rate and breathing returned to normal. It took another ten minutes for the shaking to stop, and twenty more before I was able to extricate myself from the airplane.

I crumpled in a heap and propped myself up against the very wheel that, had it dug into the gravel next to the runway, would have been the fulcrum around which the biplane cartwheeled itself to pieces.

"Fuck me," I breathed.

And for the first time in this journey, I questioned myself.

Eleven

I pulled off to the side of a deserted taxiway so as to not block the continuous stream of Cessna 172s emerging from the ramp to pull onto the runway and take flight. I feel the propeller blast dancing across my closed eyelids and the sun warming my upturned face. My mind is clear. My hands are still. My heart is racing. For the first time, I'm about to take to the skies in my Smith. The successful execution of this flight depends solely on me and my actions. I am very much alone. Right on cue, I feel an uncomfortably deep surging in my stomach. Pilots commonly refer to this as fear, but it's a tangled mess of that emotion, plus a thousand others. I push it down. I try to focus on the rumble of the engine and the whisper of the wind being pushed back by the propeller.

You are not alone, I tell myself.

Al had helped me strap into *DSA* that morning, and countless others strapped in with me: my flight instructors, examiners, and friends; men like Andrew Boyd and Charlie Miller and the dozen or so I'd only exchanged emails with but who had generously shared their time, memories, and experience; my mother, my sister, and my wife, who supported me and my dream unconditionally; and, of course, my dad. My dad is in my thoughts a lot today.

A drainage ditch runs along a group of hangars at the northwest corner of the airport. A chain-link fence separates the ditch from the gravel roadway. Yesterday morning I walked along it to get to Al's hangar for taxi practice. I retraced my steps to return to the clubhouse for lunch, when I went back to the hangar for afternoon taxi runs, and when I left in the early evening. Each time, a little bird, black with red and yellow flashes on its wings, left its perch on the fence and followed me. At first, I thought I'd inadvertently come too close to its nest, but its behaviour wasn't aggressive. It merely held position about a metre above my right shoulder, singing pleasantly. This morning, it followed me again as I walked from the gate to Al's hangar, balancing itself on a very light breeze. The bird and its song seem fitting. I know my father is around.

I open my eyes. The sky is a cloudless powder blue. The engine growls, driving the propeller into a whirling, silver-laced disc. I release the brakes, and the Smith and I roll forward together.

A coward lives in every pilot, born in the moments before the flyer first takes to the skies and our constant companion until the day we fold our wings forever. Aviators must stare down the coward inside them until one or the other blinks. With time, this becomes easier and then automatic, part of the ritual of flight. The coward is a persistent adversary and keeps returning, albeit weaker. Every so often, summoned by sudden terror, an unexpected challenge, or the cascade of misfortune that is occasionally the aviator's plight, the coward returns with vigour, and the pilot has no choice but to best this rival.

This is one such moment. And yet I am more passenger than pilot. I am beyond the point of rationalizing. I know that if I succumb to the roiling waves of apprehension building inside me, I will taxi off the runway and close this chapter of my life forever. That would break me. I have no choice to make.

"*Delta Sierra Alpha* to position runway 1-5 Brampton." My voice sounds thin in my ears.

I roll out, straighten the tailwheel, and stop the airplane between the one and the five painted on the runway. We sit for thirty seconds going over everything again. I feel much like I did when I first took to the skies on my own.

"*Delta Sierra Alpha*, rolling 1-5 Brampton..." My voice again — and yet it sounds like a stranger's.

A deep breath. My left hand moves forward — slowly. It is as though I'm watching through someone else's eyes. I know it is my hand, but somehow, someone else is guiding it forward and taking the throttle with it. The engine's low moan grows to a dull roar. My other hand moves the stick forward to the stop. I can feel the airplane start to come to life around me. My feet dance on the rudder pedals, dampening out the swings to no more than a degree or two left and right.

I feel the tail lighten, then lift. I can see straight ahead now. The biplane's long nose is pointing at the end of the runway three thousand feet beyond. A glance down at the airspeed — sixty miles per hour. Truly, now, there is no turning back. The engine sounds good, and the gauges confirm that. The flying wires tremble.

Sixty-five...now seventy...

That's ten miles per hour faster than the plane's stalling speed, the velocity at which the wings can no longer generate the lift needed to defeat the pull of gravity. I ease the stick back slightly, and we're off, accelerating to ninety and climbing like a shot. We rise to seventeen hundred feet before turning to follow Highway 10 to the north. I glance over my shoulder to see Brampton's twin runways and orange-roofed hangars receding.

Holy shit! I'm flying! Holy shit! I'm flying! Holy shit! Holy shit! Holy shit!

We spend some time getting acquainted in the tentative manner of newly paired dance partners. First, some gentle turns. The biplane flies like a dream: very responsive, good roll rate, lots of rudder. Even visibility over the nose in cruise isn't too bad. We try some steep turns at sixty degrees of bank, and she goes right around like a pinwheel.

A stall, then. I bring the power off slowly and progressively pull back on the stick. The slipstream whistles as it rushes through the flying wires, and at my urging, the nose drops earthward but the wings remain level. She betrays no bad habits.

We try our hand at gliding, fly a few practice approaches on a hay-field, and then pick up the reporting point for Brampton to head back in. This is likely the busiest uncontrolled airport in the country, and today it seems as if everyone is flying. I decide to remain clear until things settle down and drone aimlessly around the countryside west of the airport. I start to settle down a bit and begin to actually enjoy the flight. I am living my dream. I am flying the airplane I pretended to fly as a toddler, the same plane I heard all those stories about.

I am flying over unfamiliar territory, and the chart I reviewed prior to taking off gave a poor depiction of the landscape unfolding beneath me. I keep the airport within sight so as to not get lost. Well to the south, Toronto seems to rise out of the blue of Lake Ontario. Between Brampton and Toronto, I can clearly see Pearson International Airport and the aluminum cloud of airliners that swarm around it. To the west and northwest, the Caledon Hills climb away from me in a series of gently rolling waves. These are the hills that saw Charlie and his mates wheel and swoop in mock dogfights decades ago. To the east and northeast, the landscape is a carpet of multicoloured farmer's fields stitched together here and there by fence lines and roads. Above all this, the Smith floats happily, guided gently by my gloved hand. The hot anxiety of the takeoff roll and climb out has faded to a warm glow. I roll my shoulders back, wiggle my toes, and flex my hands around the stick and throttle.

Nothing compares to flying in an open cockpit. The freedom of being out in the open, exposed to the elements, is obvious. The little things — how the rush of air pools in the cockpit and chafes at the back of your neck, or how your eyes water after prolonged exposure to the wind — are not. I sink easily into a reverie, imagining myself as Captain Albert Ball of the Royal Flying Corps in a Nieuport 17, scanning the Western Front for German Albatross fighters, or as Jean Mermoz at the controls of a Potez 25, valiantly threading my way through deep mountain passes of the Andes, carrying airmail from Buenos Aires to Santiago.

This plane makes it easy to imagine what life was like for aviators nearly a century ago, protected only by a leather trench coat, gauntlets, a pair of goggles, and a fragile craft of wood and fabric not unlike my own.

I think of the young Royal Flying Corps pilot, drawn from the damp misery of the trenches with promises of glory as a knight of the air. Instead, he shivered in the cold loneliness of an S.E.5a single-seat fighter, bobbing drunkenly in the thin air at eighteen thousand feet, fighting to stay awake. I think of the airmail pilot who would have followed him, chased not by an enemy fighter but violent thunderstorms, dwindling daylight, and a shrinking fuel supply. I taste the desperation as he lowers his craft slowly and unsteadily into the inky darkness of unfamiliar territory, straining his eyes for the orange smudges of flare pots outlining the landing strip. My mind turns to the swashbuckling barnstormers — aerial gypsies who called a hayfield or old horse-racing track home for a day, hopped rides for a dollar or two, and then moved on.

The uniqueness of flying an open-cockpit biplane unites us all, even across a century of flight. It was true that no one was shooting at me, I had no mail to deliver, nor passenger to carry — but the wind, sun, and sky haven't changed. If they had flown on my wing and followed me down to earth, they would have looked on this world as I would upon the face of Mars, but I couldn't help but think they would feel at home in my little biplane.

The Smith flies on. I glance down at the fuel gauge by my left knee and tap it gently with a gloved finger. It reads a quarter tank. I have roughly forty-five minutes of fuel left. I decide to return to the field to shoot some practice approaches, getting lower each time before overshooting and going around again.

I fly five of these, fitting myself in between the four or five airplanes that are constantly in the circuit. As Al has told me, the approach is best made at eighty-five miles per hour with 1,700 rpm on until the flare, when one should slowly bring the throttle back and settle into the three-point attitude. With each approach and overshoot, I grow more comfortable. On the sixth approach, I resolve to land.

There are two ways to land a taildragger: a three-point or full stall landing, where the airplane touches down on all three wheels at once, or a wheel landing, where the plane lands on its main wheels alone. Nearly every Smith pilot I've spoken to has urged me to always do three-point landings, including Al. We slide down the final approach as if on rails, into the flare, rounding out at the right height with power on. The forty-foot-wide ribbon of runway rises to meet us, and the wheels touch with a squeak.

Then the bottom drops out of everything.

I feel the little biplane heel sharply to the left, and I react with right rudder, but I am far too slow. I briefly consider slamming the throttle forward and trying to power my way out, but it's far too late. We're already bounding off the runway and onto the grass beyond.

"Oh, God," I breathe, barely hearing the words over the furious pounding of my heart.

The engine replies with a gentle, almost admonishing, purr. I move the controls and watch as they respond. I glance over my shoulder and follow the tire tracks through the grass back to the runway. They run neatly between two runway lights. I collect myself before taxiing back onto the runway and into a clear taxiway.

We pass an old fellow, elbow deep in the engine of his airplane. He smiles and thumps his chest with a closed fist to simulate a beating heart. He laughs when I cross myself. Another quick look around: nothing bent or broken, except the ego.

I taxi back to the hangar. Al is working on his motorcycle. He saw the whole thing. "Man, you got lucky," he says, grinning. "You looked great right until she went for a walk. You needed a bit of right brake and she would've straightened right up."

At this point, I'm not nervous or frightened anymore. I'm not even relieved. I mangled the landing, yes, but we flew. We flew! Some of Al's hangar neighbours come over, introduce themselves, speak enthusiastically about the Smith, and offer words of encouragement about my imperfect landing.

"You can't let her get away from you, Jon," Al says soberly. "Someone was looking after you, for sure." I think of the bird and of my dad.

I walked back to the airport parking lot alone that day. The bird, his job done, was gone, and even though my ears were ringing in the aftermath of my first open-cockpit flight, I could still hear his song.

☉

It would be two long, anxious weeks before I returned to pick up my biplane and fly her to her new home at Rockcliffe. I watched the weather for ten days, trying to read the patterns in the hopes of predicting which day would provide me with the best conditions. I even asked my colleague, our local weatherman, for advice. He shrugged.

Eventually, I settled on Saturday, July 5, with Sunday in reserve if the weather turned, as it often does in Ontario. When Melody dropped me off at the Greyhound station, I felt a great deal of anxiety. We were expecting a child in the new year; we had our first ultrasound only the week before. The first glimpse of our baby's tiny beating heart cast the risks of this 230-mile flight across southern Ontario in a new light.

The bus station was almost deserted. A couple cuddled on a bench, a college student slept on another, and a young mother tried to soothe a sobbing baby. Someone played a ukulele that was slightly out of tune. When my dad worked in Toronto, we would drop him off here after his visits home, and the building still makes me feel sad. When the bus arrived it, too, was nearly empty. I picked a seat near the back, rested my head against the window, and let the low vibration of rubber on road lull me to sleep.

I dreamed vividly of my dad. I climb out of the back seat of the Super Decathlon after an aerobatics flight. The airplane smells of hot engine oil, aviation fuel, and sweat. I wipe my brow, lay my ball cap on the airplane's tail, and stretch out my back. My dad is standing on the other side of the airport fence, and seeing him there, I ask him if he'd like to go for a ride. He agrees, saying that it's been a while. Getting him into the airplane takes some time, but after some swearing and laughter, he's strapped in and ready to go. I talk him through starting the engine and guide him to the runway. He does the takeoff and climb out of Rockcliffe. As we turn east to follow the Ottawa River, I casually mention that I've found a Smith and, if all goes well, will bring it home to Rockcliffe soon.

I awake with a start. On the seat next to me is my cotton shoulder bag holding a change of clothes, my pilot's license, and, peeking out from the half-open flap, my cloth helmet and goggles. I pull them out. Waxed canvas, leather chin strap, and brass buckles — the crown of the earliest pilots. Mine differs only in that the ear cups house a modern headset so that I can communicate over the radio. My dad wore a white motocross helmet, a "brain bucket," which was likely a wiser choice. I bought my helmet before the biplane as a way to turn the dream into a plan, to visualize a goal. Now, it's a part of me — a badge of honour. In the depths of the bag is a tightly folded length of white silk, a scarf embroidered with my initials, another symbol of the very first aviators. It was part of a Halloween costume that my mom made for me when I was seven. I'm embarrassed to wear it, but I've brought it just the same.

The next morning, I wake up at my uncle's house early and unsettled. A thousand competing thoughts wage war in my mind, and inevitably, the body pays the price. At my aunt's insistence, I choke down a carrot muffin and a cup of good coffee; she won't allow me to leave her home without breakfast. Plus, she's quietly horrified that I plan to fly that little biplane home. Stepping outside, coffee cup still in hand, I see there isn't a cloud in the sky and perhaps just a breath of wind. It looks like I might go flying today.

My uncle drives me to the airport. He's much more reserved than his older brother was, but of late the similarities in looks and mannerisms spark a measure of sadness and longing in me. Thirty-three years earlier and about fifteen miles east, at the now defunct King City Airport, my dad and *FAM* began their journey to Rockcliffe. I miss my dad. He would have wanted to be here to see me off. As I hop out of the truck, my uncle promises to stick around until he sees me take off.

"There's nothing left to do," he says, knowing my mind is heavy with doubt and anxiety. "Fly it home."

About an hour later, I'm taxiing toward Brampton's northwest runway. It's a long, lonely ride with plenty of opportunities for second guesses and absolutely no chance to withdraw. By the time doubt has prodded me to glance over my shoulder, a plodding Cessna 172 cuts off the path to retreat.

Another 172 glides down to the runway, bounces once, and settles to earth with the finality of a vessel tired of flight. I wait for it to clear the runway before taxiing out myself. A last check, my voice weak and thin as I announce my takeoff on the radio, left hand forward, right foot down, shoulders hunched, every inch of my body determined to fly.

The takeoff roll is surprisingly short. The tail rises. I watch the edges of the runway wiggling this way and that in direct relation to the movement of my feet. More speed, more authority, swings dampening, airspeed climbing through sixty miles per hour, the little biplane now charging down the narrow strip of asphalt. We reach seventy miles per hour.

I apply only the slightest back pressure on the stick, the biplane's sole glaring incongruity. Al took it out of a surplus jet fighter. Buttons that once selected weaponry and launched the missiles now open a radio channel and fire the starter. We leap into the air, flying wires trembling, and the wind ravaging the exposed corner of the map tucked under my left thigh. My knees shake.

For today's flight, I've picked the airport at Holland Landing as a waypoint, even though it is not on our course to Rockcliffe. It's twenty-six miles to the northeast and will keep me well clear of the busy airspace around Toronto. Nearly a decade ago, I learned to fly taildraggers at Holland Landing. My dad watched as I went around the patch, each landing more steady and confident than the last, until my instructor cut me loose. I remember Dad beaming with pride as I taxied in from the first solo and how excitedly we swapped stories on the drive home.

The land beneath me is utterly foreign. For two weeks, I've pored over the charts meant to represent this small parcel of Ontario, but I'm having trouble matching the map to what I'm seeing outside. The bare bones are there: the gridwork of major roads, the hatched squiggle of a railway line passing through tiny dots representing the towns of Caledon East and Palgrave. The map fails to show the detail and richness of colour that I can see in the land beneath me. This is certainly not the first time I've used a map to navigate through the air, but I realize instantly how an open cockpit changes your perception. It sharpens details, brightens colours, and gives you a sense of great speed and vastness. When taken together, it makes the land below look almost foreign. I continue northeast, entirely enthralled by the mosaic of fields, fences, towns, ponds, and rivers passing beneath me.

I glance at my compass. For hundreds of years, sailors, aviators, and explorers have set their course by this marvellous instrument. Mine spins drunkenly left and then right, indicating anything from north to east and sometimes beyond. I decide to average the oscillations to fly my planned course of 050°. A few minutes later, I pull the map from under my thigh, look down over the side, and happily identify Highway 9, which will lead me to Newmarket. The airport at Holland Landing lies midway between the town and the southern tip of Lake Simcoe to the north. The sky is a violently bright blue. Visibility is perfect. Right on cue, Newmarket and Lake Simcoe appear over the horizon.

I try to imagine what the landscape would have looked like when my dad embarked on this journey in the summer of 1981. Toronto is far to the south. Airliners hover like gnats over the vast concrete patch that is Pearson International Airport. To the north and east, stretches a collection of patchwork fields and lakes dotted with hamlets, towns, and small cities.

Ten minutes later, I am perplexed. Newmarket lies behind me over my right shoulder and Lake Simcoe over my left. Holland Landing Airpark has eluded me. I bank steeply into a tight 360-degree turn, and the airstrip reveals itself exactly where it should be. The Smith's long nose hid its presence, and I'd flown directly over top of it. The fingertip of Lake Simcoe seems to mockingly point directly to the airport.

I fly a quick orbit around the field and set the heading for Peterborough. My meticulously planned flight calls for a course of 090°, but the compass can't decide which way we're heading. As we bob on the current of a strong wind out of the west, it is nearly impossible to average out the wild swings. I compare the chart to what I can see over the side. Highway 7A stretches in segments to the horizon, and my chart assures me it will lead us straight to Peterborough.

There's a great liberty in picking a highway and following it to your destination, a certain magic in pulling out your chart that evening, still tingling in the afterglow of flight, a cup of coffee and a half-eaten sandwich serving as paperweights, and tracing an oil-stained finger along your path, discovering the names of the places you flew over. You might discover you've been there before, by car or plane, and you might be shocked to realize how different it looks from an open cockpit. You've never seen greens, golds, cobalts, and rusts until you've seen them from a thousand feet on fabric twin wings that quiver in the rush of air.

Some twenty minutes later, Lake Scugog drifts by. Looking down at the people living on the island in the middle of the lake, I envy them the peace and isolation they must enjoy, and then I reconsider. I'm entirely alone, a half mile above the earth, in a conversation between engine and slipstream. Below me are emerald fields dotted with multi-coloured roofs and blue pools, and above me is a sapphire sky spoiled only by my plane. I am the one to be envied. I let out a cheer. It is swept away instantly.

I pick out the Peterborough airport. My dad and I landed here about seven years ago on a Sunday circuit of local airports. It has evolved since then. When my dad landed his Smith here, the shorter, intersecting runway was still turf. Today, work crews are finishing the paving job.

I sweep into the circuit, glancing over the side to see the windsock stiff out of the west. I throttle back, roll into the base turn, briefly level the wings to check the extended final approach, and then turn directly to the threshold. A small river flashes by, then a stand of trees bent in deference to the wind, and more than a mile of asphalt stretches out before me. I round out into the flare and settle her down. I gently reduce the power and feel the lift spill from the wings. The little biplane settles onto the runway with a chirp and begins a swing to the right. I react automatically with a stab of my left foot. We roll to a stop and the world is still.

I taxi clear of the runway, shut down on the ramp, and gas up. I chat with the fuel guy. Half a dozen pilots want to take pictures and have a look inside. One abandons a brand-new, state-of-the-art plane and her new owner to tell me he once owned a little biplane like mine. His eyes twinkle when he talks about it, and he asks about my approach speed and how squirrelly she is on pavement. After a few moments, we exchange names and a handshake, and he returns to the shiny, composite, parachute-equipped Cirrus without enthusiasm. Next, I meet a student pilot flying his first solo trip from Toronto Island to Muskoka, then Peterborough and back again. He's anxious and expresses some concern about dealing with gusty winds. I confess that this is my second landing in an airplane I had to teach myself to fly. We will soon fly off in different directions and are unlikely to meet again, but we are brothers.

My cousin Michael walks out of the terminal. He's an aviation student at Seneca College, now based at the airport. When he was a little boy, my dad would go through old aviation magazines and books with him and stoke his dreams of flight. It wasn't long before Michael could identify the airliners flying overhead. Soon after, he was flying them halfway around the world, albeit by computer simulator. Like me, he joined the air cadets as soon as his age allowed. A few years later, he earned his wings as well.

Michael and I talk for more than an hour and a half. We look over the charts and briefly discuss the pros and cons of flying southeast to Kingston to refuel before turning northeast for home. The choice is not an easy one. Between Madoc to the east and Perth lies nothing but sixty miles of forest, swamp, rocks, and a few lakes. Between Kingston and Perth are only lakes, and I am not a strong swimmer. In the end, we decide I should follow Highway 7. It's the same route my father took so many years ago.

And so, at 2:15 p.m., the Smith and I clatter into the sky above Peterborough, turn right, and pick up the highway. A brisk tailwind shepherds me east, and in no time at all I see the inactive airstrip at Norwood, its gravel runway overrun by grass and brush and its hangars stand empty. Norwood was an active place until its former owner died in a plane crash near the strip. Now, trailers litter the grounds. But the new owner leaves the runway clear for pilots who ask for permission to use it in advance.

In a flash, the strip is gone. I fly over Havelock with a cluster of three lakes to the north and, to the south, the Trent River. Far to the south, the navigational aid at Campbellford fires invisible beams out from its centre, like spokes on a wheel. Other airplanes can latch onto these signals and follow them to far-off places. I can see no companions, although at regular intervals, I hear another pilot on the radio, reporting their position over another town or lake. They are never nearby, but I hear them with such clarity. I am very much alone and content to fly in silence.

Next comes Marmora, Deloro, and finally Madoc, with a lake to the south my chart has named Moira. It's a pretty name for a lake. Two small boats play on her surface. In their wake, they leave winding tails that twist and tangle, threaten to bump into one another and, at the very last instant, separate in a spray of pure white speckles.

Up until this point, I've made regular position reports over each town, announcing to radar stations on the ground our identity, position, height, and destination. I imagine a room with someone bathed in the light of a bare bulb, cigarette smoke clinging grimly to the ceiling, peering at the glow of the radar screen. I am without a transponder, an ingenious little piece of technology that automatically relays our type, course, speed, and altitude. We appear on what is known as primary radar only as an echo. My position reports give the slow-moving blip on the controller's screen a name and a voice.

Soon I won't bother with the position reports. They know who I am and where I am going. Calling out routine reports over the radio only serves to heighten my sense of isolation. My attention is best paid to the engine instruments and watching for the town of Carleton Place, which will mark our return to civilization. We are crossing an invisible line into what is the most unsettling part of our trip, at least for me. For the next sixty miles, the seemingly endless landscape of trees, rocks, and swamps repeats itself. If the engine quits, I'll have precious few choices, each one poorer than the last. I pull the biplane's nose up and gain another thousand feet, so if the unthinkable should happen, the added height will buy me an extra thirty seconds, maybe a minute.

Every fifteen seconds, my eyes scan the engine instruments for any sign of trouble. The engine does not betray me: the oil pressure has stood resolute at eighty pounds per square inch since we left Peterborough, its temperature at seventy-five degrees. It has remained so for my entire time in this airplane, and for 575 hours before that, and roughly a thousand more during the ten years when this engine pulled a little Piper taildragger around the sky.

Puffy bands of cumulus clouds have now appeared on the horizon and inch toward us. Every so often, we are cast in shadow as one passes overhead. On the ground below, darker patches dot the landscape, matching the overhead march of the clouds. They look like islands in a sea of green. One out of every four clouds is ringed in a translucent silver halo, backlit by a sun arcing to the west, behind us.

I suddenly want to know exactly where I am and, by a simple calculation, to discover how far I've left to go and how fast (or slow) my progress has been. I pull the chart from under my thigh and discover that I've flown off the edge. I need to unfold the map and refold it to reveal the next part of the trip. Al has warned me that this is no easy feat in a single-seat open cockpit. I thought he might have been exaggerating. He was not. At once, the map, formerly folded into a neat rectangle, billows like an angry cloud in the small cockpit. My gloved hands abandon the stick and throttle and try to jam the map back into a manageable shape. The left wing drops and the Smith claws into a climbing turn. I look out and am alarmed to see nothing but blue skies and a single cumulus cloud. Right elbow down on the map, left arm tight against my body, I wear the map like a towel as I grab the stick and return us to straight and level flight.

The engine races. I stretch a finger and hook the throttle back. I consider letting the map go — *to hell with you* — but Al told me his once leapt from the cockpit and wrapped itself around the brace wires that hold the tail together. The drag caused such an alarming rattle in the stick that he landed at the first airport he saw, which was fortunately located just below him. I don't need the map to tell me that the only airport within thirty miles of me is Tomvale, somewhere to the north, and I wouldn't be able to find it without the map. I spend the next few minutes wrestling with the airplane and the map, alternately, before I manage to roll the map into a tightly crumpled cylinder I can jam under my thigh for the rest of the flight.

The wind swirls around the cockpit, tugging at my shoulders and buffeting the loose chinstrap of my cloth helmet. As my heart rate subsides and my breathing returns to normal, I realize how calm and peaceful it is inside the tiny cockpit, despite the ferocity of the slipstream sliding along the airplane's fabric flanks. Soon, the vast forests give way to fields and pastures, and the pack of lakes that have been constant companions off my right wing come to an end. I spot Perth, where I passed through yesterday on the bus. Here, I'll turn northeast and cross Mississippi Lake.

The small grass strip at Carleton Place creeps past my left shoulder. The airfield is quiet and only a scattering of small airplanes stand guard. When my dad landed his Smith here, the airport still bore Perth's name. I briefly consider swooping down for a landing, but the windsock indicates a stiff wind across the airport's only runway. Given I've only had one successful landing in this airplane, I decide to leave howling crosswinds for another day. Beyond the airport to the north lies the town of Carleton Place. A century ago a young man bent on joining the First World War in the air left his home here, took lessons at the school founded by the Wright brothers themselves, and then volunteered for service with Britain's Royal Navy Air Service. Three years later, Captain A. Roy Brown was credited with bringing down Manfred von Richthofen, the famed Red Baron, in a sugar beet field in northern France. Brown later said he could not have felt more sorrow if he had killed his best friend.

In another twenty miles, I reach the airport at Carp, where my dad parked his Smith while he arranged her permanent home at Rockcliffe. Before us now lies Constance Lake, lined by angry whitecaps that march like an army across her dark grey face. Here, in the skies above this lake, my dad and I flew our final flight together.

We continue east, cross the Ottawa River, emerge on the Quebec side, perhaps a quarter mile north of the Ottawa navigational aid, and cross the Gatineau hills south of Camp Fortune. This is now familiar territory, airspace I regularly ply when I'm teaching others to fly aerobatics. The Chelsea Dam sits balanced on the propeller hub, with the Gatineau airport beyond. A little to the east, framed by the right-hand cabane strut, is Rockcliffe.

My first call to the ground station at the old air force base — really just a radio atop the dispatcher's desk — is an emotional one. My voice is cracking. It's been a long journey: three hours in the air and a decade, if not more, in the making. This first landing at Rockcliffe will be both an exclamation mark and an ellipsis, both an end and a beginning. The dispatcher confirms that winds are strong and gusty out of the west. The runway, however, is wide and familiar. I sweep overhead, cut the power back, and carve a descending U-shaped turn to return across the field at circuit height. The Miniplane is no glider and gleefully bleeds altitude. Two turns later, I look down the length of Rockcliffe's historic airstrip. A few moments pass, and the first Smith Miniplane since *Foxtrot Alpha Mike* more than thirty years ago comes home to Rockcliffe.

For a brief, uplifting instant, I believe Dad is down there waiting for me, sitting on the old bench outside the clubhouse or pouring a cup of coffee in the pilot's lounge. What would Dad think of me bringing another Smith to this field? Then, in the next moment, I remember he's gone. And yet he's here. In the small baggage compartment behind my head are his pilot's licence and logbook. I brought them along, too, so that, in some way, he could fly this trip with me.

The runway rushes up to meet us. We've flared slightly high and now we're dropping. A burst of power and the descent is arrested. We touch down on all three points and hop into the air again. At the second time of asking, she stays earthbound, and we roll to a stop abeam the first taxiway.

We're home.

Twelve

My early flights in the Smith were like riding the old bike of my child-hood. The signposts were farther away, and the distance was measured not in feet but miles, but I felt the same sense of accomplishment at reaching each self-imposed challenge. At first, I flew to the east, fol-lowing the Ottawa River, past Gatineau on the left wing and Orleans on the right, to a narrow strip of forest and farmer's fields. Here, I practised steep turns, tilting the plane onto one wing and whipping it around, as though my wingtip were balanced carefully on a farmhouse or intersection below. As my starting point crept back into view, I reversed my roll, helped the nose down, and swept elegantly through another orbit.

I followed the turns with the lazy-eights my father had taught me to fly, carving long, graceful, climbing lines into the endless sky. We climbed, pulse quickening and the slipstream fading, to that lonely apex where the wings seem to part the horizon. Then down, down, down the long, soft slope. The earth rushed up to meet us. The engine called; the slipstream answered. The flying wires hummed their own tune. I craned my neck around the windshield and thrust my face into the onslaught of wind and speed and sound. My face was a mask of determination — an immovable rock against the mighty force of the wind.

The air was shockingly cool. A deep breath was both painful and pleasant. I couldn't help smiling. A smooth movement of the right hand and deft adjustment of the right boot, and the earth fell away again. Up, up, and up into the blue, that intoxicating, hanging pause, and then down again.

A tiny voice called out. It has many names, but on that day I called it Doubt. "Enough fun for today," it chided. I protested. The sky was clear and the fuel plentiful.

An admonishing silence was Doubt's reply.

Doubt had a point. Revelling too long can make a pilot complacent, neglectful, or even careless. Best to quit while I was ahead.

We turned westward and eased into a dive, racing for home. In a few minutes, Rockcliffe Airport presented itself. The winds were as they were when we departed: a gentle sigh out of the west. A trio of tin-can trainers plied the circuit, dutifully announcing their positions in the wide carousel. I fit myself in as best I could, mindful of staying close to the field and going slow enough to not upset the rhythm of the pattern.

This was my fourth approach in my Smith.

The sound of the engine making 1,700 rpm.

Eighty mph on the airspeed indicator.

The comforting aroma of doped fabric.

Rockcliffe's single runway unfurled over the nose.

The clockwork ticking of my heart.

The runway rising.

Wires whistling.

Is that Fear? No, it's Doubt once more.

A jolt and then stillness.

I glanced at my watch. Thirty-six minutes had passed since I switched on the engine. I never tire of the wonder I feel when I consider that we can assign such a specific number to an experience that feels like both a few ecstatic heartbeats and a wistful eternity. The Smith and I were beginning to understand one another. She had much to teach me but, as with that old bicycle, I had passed my first lesson. Tomorrow we'd add another step, and then another.

As my ease grew, so did the Smith's. When I relaxed my grip on the stick, I felt the tension melt out of her and fall away through the summer heat. Her wings bit into the thin air with such a ferocity that I felt she was happy to be bobbing about in her natural element. The propeller took greedy gulps of new air, driving us forward with each pass of its blades. The flying wires hummed and whistled a tune in harmony with the engine's bass track. All was right with the world.

But if I lingered too long while orbiting a small town, or if I touched down with too much speed and skipped back up into the air, I felt her bristle, as though I'd allowed her to recall that it was no longer Al's hand guiding her but mine.

We began again, anew, each time, and the education was nothing short of a love affair.

These summer days came in two variants: the first, warm and clear under a perfect blue sky; the second, heavy with sweat and steam. The mist hung like a curtain and made the most familiar landmarks seem alien. On these days, I stayed close to the field to practise takeoffs and landings. I very rarely stayed up for more than three or four circuits. The Smith's short, stubby wings made it a poor glider. We had to stay very close to the airport in order to make it back if the engine quit. The Smith's poor gliding capability meant our approach speed was faster than most airplanes. A standard circuit in a training airplane like the Cessna 172 lasts about five or six minutes. The Smith's were half as long, and so my workload to set the airplane up for landing was high.

Everything happened faster in the Smith than in other airplanes I had flown. Andrew Boyd, who had prepared me to fly her, had said it best: "Flying these things is easy; the hard part is fitting into the circuit and landing." Each flight progressed in the same manner: my first landing was always tentative, the second was always a marked improvement on the first, the third was perhaps the best of them all, and the fourth was so humbling it persuaded me to call it a day. I always emerged from the Smith's cockpit soaked in sweat, as much from exertion as from the heat.

On the warm, clear days, I would pick a direction and endeavour to discover what lay on the far side of the nearest horizon. The airspace above major cities with large airports is complex and tightly controlled. Airplanes sharing the sky with passenger traffic around these major centres need transponders to supply key information to air traffic controllers. The Smith didn't have a transponder on board, and so a southerly heading toward Ottawa's international airport wasn't possible. Still, that left us with the three remaining cardinal directions.

On one such foray east, somewhere between Orleans and Rockland, I suddenly thought of Jean-Pierre Seguin, a friend and aerobatic student I hadn't seen much of lately. He was spending most of his summer installing solar panels on the roof of his barn. But I remembered him telling me his farmhouse was in this area and across from a large field where, years ago, he once landed an Aeronca Champ. I looked over the side and under my left main wheel saw, much to my amazement, a large barn covered in solar panels. I swung my head over the other side and spied a large field where a small plane could certainly land. Then I saw a red van, just like the one Jean-Pierre drove, winding down the long gravel lane that led to the barn and farmhouse. I swung around into a tight orbit.

I rolled the Smith out of the turn, drew the throttle back, and shed a few hundred feet as I swung around again for another pass. The van was parked, half in the barn's shadow. I was sure I could see a tiny figure far below and imagined Jean-Pierre shading his eyes against the August sun, gazing up at this little airplane and its movements that were too precise to be chance alone.

I waggled my wings, clawed into a wingover, returned for another pass, and again waggled my wings in greeting. I hoped Jean-Pierre was standing next to that van and not some stranger likely to be puzzled, even annoyed, by the barnstorming fool in their backyard.

When I returned to Rockcliffe and dug my phone out of my jacket, a series of enthusiastic text messages from Jean-Pierre validated my hunch.

One early evening I flew north, up the Gatineau River toward Chelsea, Quebec, at the urging of a colleague who wanted me to see his new house. He showed me where he lived on a map and told me to look for a dock with two red kayaks.

An hour later, the Smith and I launched into the early evening sky. We made a slight turn to the north and climbed to seventeen hundred feet. The Gatineau River, at least on that evening, was a wide blue slash through the southern extremity of the Canadian Shield. The Smith and I droned up the river valley, careful to stay within gliding distance of a field in case of engine trouble.

I passed over the float-plane base at Chelsea. I found my target: a dock with two bright-red kayaks. I made a few passes over the dock and the house but failed to rouse any response below. Intent on making the most of this flight, I continued up the valley, first to Chelsea and then Wakefield.

Wakefield holds a special place in my heart. When we were little, our parents took Vanessa and me to a freshwater spring to collect water nearly every weekend until my dad began working out of town. I remember the clang the metal trap door made when my dad threw it open and how the sound echoed down the cavernous mouth of the spring. I remember the strength of the water's gush and how cold it felt when my dad, one arm wrapped around my waist, allowed me to lean forward into the void. The drive to the spring was long and winding before the highway was built, and we passed a number of gas stations with old-fashioned pumps. I remember the hiss of the old train engine that once ran a length of track through town and the taste of warm apple crumble with vanilla ice cream that they used to serve in the restaurant in the old station.

More than two decades later, Melody and I honeymooned at the Wakefield Mill, eating our fill of steak frites and spending too much on red wine and single malt scotch. We'd walk down to the village and along the old railway tracks, jumping like kids from rotting tie to tie. Every once in a while, my ears picked up the familiar, throaty hum of an airplane's engine, and I turned my face skyward and squint, searching.

Looking down now, I wondered if anyone heard the sound of my engine and was searching the sky for me.

My eyes caught the iconic covered bridge at Wakefield. Built in 1915, destroyed by fire in 1984, and rebuilt more than a decade later, it was one of the region's most photographed landmarks. From my vantage point, it appeared as little more than a collection of crimson matchsticks. I turned south and flew over my colleague's home again. After a few orbits, he walked down the dock. I waggled my wings, and I'm certain he waved his arms in reply. Another pass, another friendly dip of the wings, and I rattled off for home.

The westerly flights were long, lazy tours. They involved shooting a narrow alley between the Ottawa navigational beacon and the communications tower crowning the ski hill at Camp Fortune before turning northwest and skirting the Gatineau Hills escarpment. I often called on the drag strip at Luskville and the now-abandoned fly-in community at Pontiac before climbing and crossing the river into Ontario. Here, the Smith and I plied the skies over Dunrobin Road from Constance Bay to Constance Lake before turning east for home.

I'd spent more than ten years flying in these parts, but in the Smith I felt as though I was viewing this landscape for the first time. The simple beauty of the quilt of fields always impressed me. When the sun is high in the sky, the greens, browns, and golds shimmer with intensity. As the sun dips and the shadows grow, the colours deepen.

Balanced on the wind, I have seen and understood the magnificence of our world, just as my father did before me.

Thirteen

Our inaugural open-cockpit flying season slipped away. The days became shorter with each sunset, and the warmth was drained from the air. It grew chilly and then cold. T-shirts and shorts turned into light sweaters and long pants, and then an insulated jacket, long underwear, and joggers. Eventually, my sheepskin gloves and a balaclava came out.

The winds stirred and strengthened. The clouds were thicker in the weightier air. The wind blew mostly out of the west. The Ottawa River deepened from blue to grey. The Gatineau Hills slowly aged from green to a breathtaking mosaic of every conceivable hue of brown, red, yellow, and orange. And then, there were no leaves at all, only naked trees on the muddled brown hills.

The changes exposed elements I'd never seen before or had forgotten about: a rocky outcropping springing from the side of a hill and plunging down its face like a silvery waterfall frozen in time, an old yellow school bus, tinged in rust, abandoned in a stand of trees.

The Smith took what I saw as a slow, bittersweet death and turned it into a rebirth. Invigorated by the cooler, denser air, she leapt into the sky and climbed like a homesick angel. The forty-year-old engine sounded like it had rolled off the assembly line at Williamsport, Pennsylvania, the week before. The stubby wings cleaved the thick air with renewed vigour and buoyed the plane and her pilot on a rising tide of autumn air.

While the Smith was content to keep climbing to her service ceiling of thirteen thousand feet and very likely beyond, the cold meant I almost always pulled on the reins around two thousand feet. The loss of even a degree or two at altitude made a shockingly painful difference. The wind burned my skin and made my eyes ache. My breath froze into tiny beads of ice that tangled in my beard. While I was exposed to the elements, the blast of the propeller and the weight of the air rushing past created something of a capsule against the outside world. The engine's roar eventually subsided into a dull, monotonous hum. The silence was eerie. After each flight, as I shivered in front of the clubhouse's electric stove, I told myself that it would be the last of the season. Inevitably, I'd find an excuse to launch again a few days later. I didn't want the season to end.

I had a secondary reason for not liking to fly above two thousand feet. At not quite sixteen feet long and eighteen feet wide, the Smith is unquestionably a miniature plane. The few times I took her up to four thousand feet it felt as though we were in orbit. At that height, peering over the side made me dizzy. It was a lonely, humbling and, at times, frightening experience that emphasized my insignificance.

The Smith was impervious to my fears. After all, she'd crossed half the continent and vaulted the Northumberland Strait at a height that made me nervous.

I still routinely spent twenty minutes — sometimes more — standing outside the hangar, rocking gently from foot to foot, watching each of the three windsocks in the same way a surfer gauges the waves before paddling out beyond the break. On some days, having rolled up the doors, pulled out the flying club's Super Decathlon I teach aerobatics with, prepared the Smith, and made it ready for flight, I would sigh resignedly and do everything again in reverse.

"A plane isn't a car," my dad had said to me once, a long time before I started flying. "You can't just pull over if something goes wrong."

It was true. In the best-case scenario, you found an airport or field to land in as soon as practical; in the worst case, if there was no clearing, you made one.

Here I am landing the Smith at Rockcliffe Airport. In the background, newly minted Royal Canadian Air Cadets practise for the "Wings Parade" where they'll receive their wings in front of friends and family who couldn't attend the formal ceremony. (Photograph courtesy of Chuck Clark)

Above the toilet of the flying school where I did my night rating, commercial license, and aerobatic training, hung a yellow poster bearing the image of a burned-out Curtiss "Jenny" biplane hanging in a blackened tree and Captain Alfred Gilmer Lamplugh's widely known and reproduced observation: "Aviation in itself is not inherently dangerous. But to an even greater degree than the sea, it is terribly unforgiving of any carelessness, incapacity or neglect." Every time I saw the poster, I read that quote and took in the image. Only the airplane's rear fuselage and tail remained. The tree appeared to be the only obstacle for miles. Every time I looked at that poster, I thought of the pilot and wondered what had happened. I approached every flight I ever made with self-examination. Am I ready? Am I safe? Am I prepared? Am I able to handle what may come? Do I have a way out?

If the answer to any of those questions was no, I went home, poured myself a drink, and toasted Captain Lamplugh.

By the time of our last flight of our first season, we had logged a little more than twenty-two hours aloft. Each minute had been an investment and a learning experience. The last flight, on November 11, was meant only to warm the oil enough so that it would be easier to drain from the engine. I took the biplane out to the other side of Orleans, circled Jean-Pierre's farm twice, and returned to Rockcliffe. My landing was perhaps our nicest of the season, and as I taxied back to the hangar, I marvelled at the Smith's grace. I felt that my little plane knew I'd had an exhilarating, challenging, emotional season and had decided to reward me.

Seamus Reid, my best friend since childhood, helped me drain the Smith's oil and replace it with preservative fluid for her winter hibernation. We carried out some minor corrosion prevention work and removed the battery from its case, an old ammunition box welded to the steel tubing behind the pilot's seat. We worked slowly and in silence, our labour a solemn veneration to the passing of the season. It was dusk by the time we had her back together and tucked into the corner of the hangar. The Super Decathlon followed suit. I rolled down the doors and tied them up.

A peaceful silence covered the field as I walked back to the clubhouse. The only sounds I could hear were my breath and the soft scraping of my boots on the crumbling pavement. Anyone who has spent any time at an airport will tell you that quiet moments are rare. Windsocks rustling, engines coughing to life before settling into a rhythmic purr, the clang of a wrench, a backfire, the rattle of a kid hanging off the perimeter fence, happy greetings shouted across the ramp — this is the soundtrack of an airport like Rockcliffe.

And yet, tonight there was none of that. Not a whisper. Not a breath besides my own.

The clubhouse was nearly empty. The dispatcher worked behind the desk, updating journey logs that chronicled a busy day of flying.

We chatted idly as I rummaged through the cash box looking for one of my instructing paycheques. Two men, whom I assumed to be the pilot and passenger of a Cessna sitting outside, loitered by the rack of snacks the club offered for sale.

"Everything's a dollar?" one asked me. He had a pair of aviator sunglasses pushed up on his forehead.

"Yep," I replied, scribbling down the particulars of today's flight and oil change in the Smith's journey log.

"I'll take a Snickers."

"Help yourself."

I snapped the log shut, dug my car keys out of my mailbox, said goodnight to the dispatcher, nodded to the Cessna crew, and stepped out into the November night.

When I arrived at the newsroom early the next morning, messages about a small plane crash in Algonquin Park crowded my email inbox. The Cessna 150 was on its way from Rockcliffe to Buttonville with two people on board when it issued a distress call at around eight thirty the night before. They were lost in deteriorating weather with their fuel running low. An Air Canada flight picked up their call for help and relayed it to the Joint Rescue Coordination Centre at Canadian Forces Base Trenton. A Hercules airplane and Griffon helicopter responded while the Air Canada crew tried to keep the pilot calm.

They made their last radio call at 9:28 p.m., almost three-and-a-half hours after departing Rockcliffe, which lay only an hour and a half's flying to the east. When the crash site was located, a search-and-rescue technician confirmed that the pilot and passenger were dead. They were, of course, the two who had been in the clubhouse the evening before. I felt sick.

I wondered why anyone would embark on that kind of flight. A light, single-engine aircraft crossing the dark, unforgiving expanse of Algonquin Park in strong winds and deteriorating weather at night was at best a bad idea. The tragic result was almost inevitable. I'd flown over the relatively well-populated southern extremes of that area before, in daytime, and was struck by its inhospitality. If I'd known where they were going, I'd have suggested staying the night or, if they absolutely had to go, recommended heading southwest to Kingston and then following the lights of Highway 401. Would they have listened?

The Transportation Safety Board's final report on the crash was gut-wrenching. The pilot and passenger thought they were flying southwest toward home, but thanks to a malfunctioning instrument, they were flying west, deeper into Algonquin Park. The pilot descended, likely to try to keep the ground in view, and the Cessna's propeller struck a twenty-foot-tall tree. Both men survived the impact and were able to get out of the cockpit, but they died soon afterwards. One of the cellphones on board had GPS capability that, had it been turned on, would have been able to pinpoint the aircraft's location and potentially guide them to safety.

I was six years old when I first saw an airplane take a pilot's life. It was Canada Day in 1990, and my dad and I were sitting on a little knoll overlooking the Ottawa International Airport for the annual airshow. We were watching two Second World War fighters, a British Hawker Hurricane and an American P-51 Mustang, chase each other across a clear sky. We had seen the Mustang up close the day before — it was big and mean with a yellow-and-black checkerboard tail. Her red nose bore the Grim Reaper brandishing a scythe and the words *Death Rattler.*

With an angry growl from her Merlin engine, the Mustang soared skyward into a manoeuvre known as a wingover — really one half of a lazy-eight where the aircraft banks vertically before sliding earthward again and reversing course. At the apex of the manoeuvre, the Mustang seemed to stagger before rolling hard to the left to finish pointing straight down. Even as a boy, I knew that this was not part of the act. My dad tensed, sitting bolt upright.

"Pull out of it," he whispered. "Pull out of it."

The crowd around us stirred uneasily. A few voices cried out in alarm. The airplane continued its plunge.

"He's not going to make it." My dad's voice was calm, almost matter-of-fact.

The Mustang disappeared behind a line of trees. A puff of black smoke followed by a soft thump signalled the outcome.

I've had a few acquaintances die in plane crashes. There's one in particular I think of quite often. We had met at the air cadet gliding school in Trenton, Ontario, in the summer of 2005. I was replacing him as the unit's public affairs officer and he spent a week showing me the ropes.

He died in the early evening on a snow-covered plateau in the northeastern part of British Columbia, just east of the Fort St. John airport that was supposed to be his final destination. The last night of November 2011 was cold but clear with a strong breeze blowing out of the southwest. A high ceiling of clouds hid most of the moon and shrouded the land below. He was alone in the plane, a six-seat Cessna taildragger used for aerial survey, at the end of a long day of flying. He began a gentle descent twenty-three miles from the airport and made a last call to the airport for information on the winds and runways in use. He levelled off roughly fifteen miles out before beginning his descent anew. He was only twelve miles or so from the airfield when he hit a group of trees and then the ground. He was thirty years old.

A phenomenon known as the black hole effect may have played a part in his crash. On moonless or overcast nights over water or dark, featureless terrain (like the land over which he was flying), where the only visual cues are lights on or near the airport, the pilot can have the impression that the airport is closer than it actually is and that the aircraft is therefore too high. In response, the pilot can descend too soon or too quickly, either making the approach below the correct flight path or hitting the ground short of the runway.

He was not only an experienced and skilled pilot but one of those rare people who is genuinely a friend to everyone. We didn't know each other well, but he was kind to me when I was starting a job in an intimidating place where I knew few people, and his death affected me deeply. Every so often, I come across a picture or a social media post, and I'm taken back to a beach on Lake Ontario. He's standing in the warm light of a giant bonfire fed by pilfered aviation fuel, offering a cold beer with an outstretched hand and a mischievous smile.

Fourteen

Open-cockpit planes don't typically fly in Canadian winters, and their pilots inevitable lose a degree or two of skill, comfort, and confidence during the long months on the ground. Dad often spoke of the challenge of essentially retraining himself to fly his Smith each spring. The only option, we both discovered, is to open the throttle, throw caution to the wind, launch into the wild blue yonder, and hope you and your plane will come back in one piece.

The extended break from flying my own Smith wasn't the only reason I started our second season feeling like a bit of a novice. I'd had a turbulent winter.

In 2014, the network that had employed me for almost ten years had embarked on a major restructuring that cut eighty positions. Just two days before my thirty-first birthday, I found myself out of work for the first time in fifteen years. The truth was that journalism had lost its lustre, and I had almost made up my mind that it was time for a change: my career was unlikely to advance further if I stayed in Ottawa, and I didn't want to leave. What's more, I had stopped learning. This, however, did not make the layoff any easier. In the weeks that followed, I felt anger bordering on white rage and then deep sadness. One colleague tried to console me by telling me the layoff wasn't personal. Not personal? The network had ended my career, eroded my self-worth, and plunged my family into uncertainty. It felt personal to me. I busied myself by submitting job applications and going to the gym, usually twice but occasionally as much as three times a day.

And then, on one of those bitterly cold January mornings when you yearn for sunlight, I trudged down a hospital corridor in the same jogging pants and T-shirt I'd been wearing for the past twenty-four hours, following Melody in a hospital bed as a nurse wheeled her around a corner. In the crook of my left arm I cradled our baby boy.

Sorry, Dad, that you can't be here to meet your grandson.

We named the baby boy Elgin and gave him the middle name Anthony after my father. I was excited to become a father, but I didn't feel quite ready. I suspect most if not all new parents feel that way, but in my case, the layoff exacerbated my doubts. I had seen what happened to my dad when his business went bankrupt. I, too, placed providing for my family above all else, and now I didn't have a job.

To my dad, being a provider meant depositing a cheque in the bank every two weeks. This was certainly important, but it seemed incomplete, even old-fashioned, to me. To me, providing for a family also meant being present. When Dad died, my biggest regret was the effect his extended absences for work had on our relationship. Holding my son in my arms reinforced the need to find paid work, but I wasn't going to sacrifice my family for a career.

When the flying season opened in April, I offered my services as a full-time aerobatic instructor to the Rockcliffe Flying Club. I'd work Wednesday through Sunday (weekends are the busiest time for flying lessons). The aerobatic program competed with the petulant April weather, with its fluctuating temperatures and sudden rain showers that often came with the fury of a monsoon. May's weather was usually more stable, and brought a stream of new and returning aerobatic students. In the short term, I planned to fill the gaps in my schedule with short jaunts in the Smith.

⊘

Transport Canada had approved me as an aerobatic instructor pilot in April 2009, and the next day, the school that trained me hired me to teach part time. Then in June 2011, I was offered the opportunity to design and lead a new aerobatic program at Rockcliffe, and I jumped at the chance. I taught on evenings and weekends around my regular journalism job until switching to out of necessity to full time in early 2015.

Unlike my dad, I really enjoyed teaching. I'd learned so much from the generous instructor pilots who strapped in next to me. After Nigel Barber came Paul "Pitch" Molnar, the former CF-18 fighter pilot who, at my dad's insistence, took me on my first aerobatic flight in a Super Decathlon atop the airport in St. Catharines. He didn't even bat an eye when I threw up after one crazed, upside-down corkscrew dive. Marc Ouellet, a former Snowbird pilot and air force colonel remained serene even when I nearly killed him twice and signed me off for solo aerobatics. Tyson Morelli taught me lazy-eights, and Tony Hunt taught me the finer points of tailwheel flying as we wrestled a Cessna 170 through a vindictive crosswind. From Andrew Campbell I learned that a great instructor knows not only what will happen, but why. Teaching gave me the opportunity to pass on what I'd learned, to improve my skills, and to fly interesting planes.

Simon Garrett was the chief pilot at Rockcliffe. Flight instruction is unique. It's the key to the health and safety of air transportation, and yet in the hierarchy of flying jobs, it resides permanently in the dank basement. Simon was one of the career instructors who not only managed to stay alive long enough to eke out something of a living, he also found a way to foster and champion pilots of all kinds, regardless of their aspirations. I'm not sure I've met a more generous and dedicated teacher.

As an aerobatic instructor, I had no formal training in teaching the basics of flight to my students, who were all qualified and licensed pilots. However, many had never flown in a tailwheel airplane. It fell to me to help them adapt their existing skills to the new kind of flying and coach them in the finer points of taking off and landing.

Eleven manoeuvres comprise the foundational aerobatic repertoire. It starts with the basic elements of loop and roll, and then introduces variations and combinations until it culminates in the pinnacle man-oeuvre: the hammerhead. This involves a brisk pull to the vertical until the wing cuts the distant horizon in half. The pilot leans on the right rudder pedal to stay straight during the pull. Once the desired angle is achieved, the pilot needs to add slight forward pressure on the stick to keep the plane from slowly turning onto her back. At this point, it's a waiting game. As the ship climbs the vertical line, gravity inevitably takes over, and her progress slows and eventually stops. The slipstream tightens around the airframe and gives the pilot a buffet, a trembling of the stick similar to what's experienced when the aircraft's engine is given a final check on the ground before takeoff. In this check, the pilot pushes the throttle forward and increases the engine's power while holding the brakes. The aircraft quivers in the same way it does at the apex of the hammerhead. At this point, some four to five seconds after the hitting the vertical line, the pilot must add left rudder to begin the pivot, right stick to hold the wing down, and slight forward pressure to keep the cut even. If executed properly, the aircraft pivots through 180 degrees and travels earthward.

There's a lot going on in the hammerhead, most of it counter-intuitive, and it all happens more or less at once. Panicky novices tend to follow the application of left rudder with left aileron (as they've been taught to through their training before aerobatics), which results in the aircraft falling out of the manoeuvre in an awkward roll. The reason for this reflex is simple: much of the physical part of flying is muscle memory. After years of flying a certain way, it takes a terrific amount of self-awareness and patience to understand manoeuvres and break habits.

Late in my first season teaching aerobatics, one of my students pulled the aircraft into a climb and briskly stopped on the line hurtling skyward. A few moments later, as the airplane gave us her telltale shudder, he replied with full left rudder and the airplane's nose began to swing left. It was as though time stopped, and I found myself thinking of how I would have felt doing this only a few short years ago during my own training. During my apprenticeship with Nigel, a mere stall or spin would drain the colour from my face and cause me to reach out for something stable to hold onto.

Flight instruction, like all teaching, is a calling. Truly, not much compares to teaching someone to fly an airplane, but not every pilot is cut out for it. For one thing, it can feel like your student is actively trying to kill you. I've twice had students freeze on the controls during spins. In the first case, I kept barking verbal commands to help the student recover from the corkscrew plunge, and he eventually snapped out of it. In the second case, I wrenched the controls away from the student and brought us out of the spin. In both cases, we had plenty of altitude and therefore plenty of time to avoid disaster, but they were sobering experiences.

Every student and every flight is different, even if I've taught the lesson two hundred times. I hardly touch the controls. Instead, I fly with my mind and my words, staying ahead of the airplane while watching over my student and critiquing their performance. Few things in aviation compare to a student's reaction when they fly upside down for the first time or finally ace a manoeuvre they've been trying to get just right.

As a kid, I loved hanging out at airports with my dad. At small, community airfields there is always more hanging around and chatting than actual flying. By the time late spring rolls around at Rockcliffe, there's always a small group of old-timers (even if they aren't very old) sitting in the shade of the gazebo, swapping flying stories and grading landings in whispers. Anthony Payison's famous burgers sizzle on his grill, in operation at the airport for decades. And if you're done flying for the day, there's a bottle of Red Stripe with your name on it in his fridge and a picnic table or lawn chair upon which to enjoy it.

A full-time aerobatic instructor has a lot of free time, especially during the week. There were gaping holes in my schedule. When they weren't spent watching airplanes take off and land or chatting with fellow pilots, I jumped in the Smith and went for a flight.

On an early summer morning, just before lunch, the Smith sat alone in the shade of the hangar. I sat a few hundred feet away, chewing thoughtfully on a protein bar. I'd just finished teaching a lesson in the Decathlon and had two hours before my next student was due to arrive. I'd added a few gallons of fuel and checked the Smith for flight earlier that morning just in case I felt like going flying. We had beautiful flying weather — letting the day pass without getting the Smith into the air would be a wasted opportunity. My biplane was imploring me to take us out for a quick trip. I swear it looked at me like a dog that simply must go for a walk that instant. The Smith might as well have been whining by the door, tail wagging, leash hanging from her jaws.

With a sigh, I hopped off the plywood box that housed wing covers, engine blankets, and tie-down ropes, and started toward the biplane. I stopped to let the Cessna 170 roll by and casually waved to the pilot. On the other side of the taxiway, I chatted briefly with another aviator. With each step, my excitement grew.

Moments later, I pushed the airplane out into the sunlight and listened to the sound of the wheels roll along the tarmac. I drummed my fingers on the taut fabric of the wings, strummed the flying wires and tail braces, and ran my hands along the leading edges, cowls, and prop. It felt good to settle into the familiar cockpit.

Belts on and locked. Helmet on and goggles up. Fuel on. Throttle set. Mixture knob forward to full rich. Three shots of primer. Master switch on. Ignition switches on. Brakes set.

I whispered the words as my eyes followed my hands around the cockpit.

Right hand on the stick, left hand resting gently on the throttle, head up, and neck craned left to look around the long nose.

"Clear!"

My pinky finger hit the starter button. The propeller turned once, twice. The engine coughed and roared to life. The Smith quivered.

Soon, we sprinted down the runway. Save for some periodic taps on the right, I hardly touched the rudder pedals. I eased off on the forward stick so that the Smith adopted a slight tail-low attitude as we approached flying speed. She broke ground of her own accord, and we began rising gently above Rockcliffe.

I hadn't decided where to go or what to do. I felt like going up to have a look around, just for the fun of it. The radio was silent and the skies were clear. We weren't particularly high, but I could still see the eastern reaches of Algonquin Park. The Smith and I considered the Gatineau River, the hills, and the flat lands beyond as our destination, but her little wings kept pulling us around east. Holding the leash, I let the biplane set the pace.

The Smith purred on faithfully, each cylinder following the one preceding it with unerring regularity. Intake, compression, power, exhaust — in that order, and a million times over, without so much as a hiccup. The wind shepherded us along at a fast clip. The airspeed hum and tremble of the flying wires betrayed a much greater velocity than the one on the indicator.

We raced along the south shore of the Ottawa River, and passed the urban sprawl of Orleans to find ourselves above an expanse of field and forest. I love this part of Canada — it has remained largely unchanged since aviation's early days, when pilots departed from and landed in fields.

I could see the pale triangular smudge of the former RCAF Station Pendleton. Here, at No. 10 Elementary Flight Training School during the Second World War, pilots trained for fifty hours on the Tiger Moth or Finch (and, later in the war, the Cornell). The field retains the triangular arrangement of runways and one of the expansive hangars, although the asphalt is in such poor shape that the tow planes and gliders that still use the field mostly stick to the grass.

At Masson-Angers, on the northern bank of the Ottawa River, we turned left to follow la rivière du Lièvre north past Beauchampville on the left bank and Buckingham on the right. The river, once used

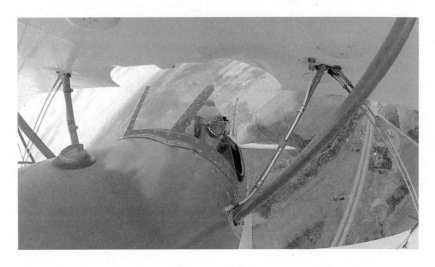

I couldn't wait to get back to flying the Smith after a long and difficult off-season. Here we are performing a wing-over manoeuvre in flight near Luskville, Quebec, on the first flight of the 2015 season.

to transport lumber downstream to the Ottawa, meanders north by northwest to the small town of Notre-Dame-de-la-Salette, where, more than a century ago, in the early morning hours of April 26, 1908, a landslide swept down the western shore of the river, taking three houses with it. Six people died. With the river blocked by mud and debris, huge blocks of ice were carried across the town, destroying a dozen more houses and twenty-five other buildings. In the end, thirty-four people were killed, roughly ten per cent of the town's population — many of them in their beds. That wasn't the only tragedy that town has seen: there had been a landslide in 1900 and another in 1912; a fire had ravaged this river town in 1903.

And maybe that's what made the air heavy — the lingering echo of catastrophes, careening off the nearby hills, swirling around the town, and rising gently into the sky above. In a different plane, free from the rush of wind and the dazzling sun, this little town and its historic shroud of sadness might go unnoticed. But here aloft where I typically enjoy focus and peace, I felt a measure of melancholy and, wrapped in it, an inexplicable eagerness to fly away. After a few more lazy spins around the village, we pointed our nose west and followed it through the hills to Poltimore, then south to Val-des-Monts before picking a valley and taking it west to Wakefield. Here, we turned south to follow the Gatineau River home.

At this point, I became aware of a faint headache. It was after one in the afternoon and the sun was strong and high in the sky. I hardly ever wore sunglasses when flying, and I'd likely been squinting for most of the flight, which was now more than an hour old. In order to feel the warm air on my face, I'd left my goggles on my forehead, and now the pressure points were burning and seemed to centre on my temples.

The circuit wasn't our best. I was sore and flushed. My head pounded, and my eyes itched. The final approach involved more power adjustment and speed chasing than usual. I just wanted to land.

We rushed over the perimeter fence and into the flare. I could have bailed out of the approach here, but I didn't. Instead, I brought the power off, and the Smith settled onto the pavement and skipped back into the air. We slid sideways for a few feet and touched down a second time before galloping into the air again. The edge of the runway hovered into view as my hands and feet worked to wrestle the biplane to the ground.

I changed my mind and opened the throttle to full. The wings, light again and invigorated, stopped the Smith from settling. With the lightest of pressure from my right wrist, we rose into the sky again and set up for another try.

"A good approach is a good landing," I heard my dad say, as clearly as though he were standing next to me, leaning up against the cockpit rim and shouting advice into my ear. He was right. That was a lousy approach. I had plenty of reasons and many chances to break off and set up again, but I chose to press it and then tried to save the landing. I broke every rule I hammered into the heads of my students. Only that morning I'd repeated my dad's words.

On the radio, I heard the pilot of the next plane in the circuit, a Cessna 172, announce that he was preparing for his final approach. Fitting into the circuit and landing is the hard part of flying the Smith. Given our respective positions, it should have worked out nicely. But the Cessna wasn't where I expected it to be.

I caught a glimpse of it gliding above a water treatment plant about two and a half miles away from the runway. Pilots generally keep the circuit within a mile of the airport so that they're able to make it back to the runway if the engine fails. I generally keep my circuits close to the field in the Smith because of its poor gliding characteristics. The Cessna's unnecessarily long approach meant I had to slow down, keep my altitude, and follow him in, which pushed me much farther away from the airport than I was comfortable with.

The Smith and I wallowed around the circuit and, once within a mile of the runway, set up to land. We crossed the airport's perimeter fence a bit faster than we should have. I let the cushion of air beneath us flatten perhaps a shade earlier than I'd aimed for and the little ship skipped back into the air. It was an unpleasant feeling — we were hanging a few feet above the asphalt with the power at idle as the scenery rushed past in a frenetic blur. I knew we were floating more than a metre above the runway. I could feel it in my seat and the heavy feeling of the wings. I knew I wouldn't damage the airplane if it fell from that height, but it would have been a wild ride down the runway. I rejected the landing and throttled up to try again.

The Smith and I played that old game where one attempts to out-wait the other. I endeavoured to keep the little biplane balanced mere inches above the pavement until the wings surrendered their lift. I was amazed at how my hands and feet operated a shade faster than my mind. I heard a squeak as the main wheels touched down and felt a little swing as the tailwheel grabbed the pavement. My feet contributed an ever-so-subtle jockeying of the pedals and the Smith rolled out straight and true.

The tension melted from my back and shoulders and a smile creased my face. I pulled my goggles up and breathed a sigh of equal parts relief and restoration. Firmly anchored to the earth again, I felt light. The seconds and minutes passed without consequence while we were aloft and while nothing had really changed, the mantle of my worries and responsibilities was not quite as heavy as it was barely an hour ago. This was the afterglow, and I wore it a little while longer still.

I tucked the Smith into the corner of the hangar, lay an apologetic hand on her cowl, and went back to the Decathlon and aerobatics.

I flew the Smith as regularly as conditions and my schedule allowed. At first, I focussed only on takeoffs and landings, concentrating on the fundamentals of speed, energy management, and power above all else. I sharpened my skills in the most critical phases of flight, shoehorning the tutelage into short intervals made even shorter by the biplane's fast approach speed.

With each flight, I became increasingly aware that I had been hurrying the airplane, forcing things to happen before they naturally should. The Smith was talking to me, teaching me to be patient again. If I did things just so, she rewarded me with a gentle touchdown and a well-behaved rollout.

Spring gave way to summer. The airplanes and their pilots grew busier. It seemed that the machines flew constantly, with only black patches of oil betraying the fact that an airplane had been in the tie-down at all. The flying club enjoyed a stream of students. A few instructors moved on to other jobs and new ones appeared, only to leave before I'd learned their names. Students shuffled around. Rockcliffe's song was one of pistons hammering away on takeoff and wings whispering as they glided down the final approach for landing.

My uniform consisted of a blue company polo shirt, sun-faded and oil-stained cargo shorts, and loafers. I wore my sweaty old Royal Canadian Air Force ball cap with pride. My skin glistened in the sun under a film of sweat and oil, and my clothes smelled of sunscreen

Fifteen

Not long after sunrise on a cool May morning, I pushed through the door of a local coffee shop. I ordered my usual — coffee with two milk and one cream (really) — took a sip to confirm that they hadn't added sugar, and shuffled to the corner table where my friends Bojan Arambasic and Ernie Szelepcsenyi were waiting for me. An aviation chart was spread out in front of them. I love maps. They promise adventure. This chart's corners were curled, and its creases were prominent and deep, and the remnants of pencil marks showed that it had helped plan many flights.

Using our coffee cups as paperweights, we traced a course on the map as we planned the morning's flight: our rendezvous point, frequencies, speeds, join procedure, break-off contingencies, safety considerations, and so on. We're going to fly in formation, Bojan and Ernie in a borrowed Cessna, and I, of course, in my Smith.

An hour later, the Smith and I clattered east across Orleans. The buckles of my leather helmet slapped against my unshaven cheeks, and the wind was rough against my face. My goggles were up and my eyes were narrow as I searched for my friends and their Cessna.

"Tally-ho!" I bellowed into the air when I saw them. (I'd always wanted to say that on an open channel but had yet to work up the courage.) I keyed my mic and asked Bojan, at the controls of the Cessna, to slow down and begin a slight turn to the right so that I could close the distance between us. A few minutes later, I slid in to the right and slightly behind the Cessna, the echelon right position.

Formation flying only works if two basic rules are met. First, the leader leads, which means they determine altitude, heading, and airspeed, as well as navigate. Second, the wingmen keep their eyes on the leader and adjust their flying to hold their position on the wing. The whole arrangement depends on absolute trust. The leader trusts his wingmen not to collide with him. The wingmen trust their leader not to fly them into the side of a mountain.

I kept my eyes on the Cessna. My hands and feet worked the stick, rudder, and throttle to keep the Smith balanced in position. Turns to the inside are relatively easy as they simply require me to slow down, while outside turns are much harder, as I must increase speed to keep pace.

Viewing another airplane in flight is nothing short of surreal. From the ground, two ships in formation appear held together by a string — rigid and unmoving relative to one another. In the air, the opposite is true. They glide along the invisible current of air, bobbing up and down and rolling left to right like two small sailboats racing across the sea.

There's only a thin line that separates fascination and terror. My first experience seeing another airplane in such close proximity happened nearly fifteen years ago by blood-chilling accident. As a result of a series of unhappy coincidences and oversights by me, the other pilot, and the flight service specialist, the other airplane ended up flying its circuit inside mine, so that we both turned final in formation completely unaware of one another. When I finally saw him, he was to my right and slightly below, in a gentle right bank. It was beautiful to behold — until the tide of terror rose. I turned left, away from the danger, flew two full circles, and let the tower know what had happened. I rejoined the approach and landed without incident. I barely made it to the bathroom before retching until my insides ached. It took a quarter of an hour for my hands to stop shaking.

Hundreds of hours later and with well-coordinated purpose, flying this close to another airplane is both a wondrous and heavy business.

I lined up the Cessna's nose and right main wheels and, through small adjustments in the throttle and precise and constant movements of stick and rudder, kept them in position. As long as those reference points remained motionless, I knew that my position relative to the leader had not changed.

Formation flying was born in the First World War, when agile fighters shepherded larger, slower, and poorly armed reconnaissance planes. In time, as tactics became more refined, fighter pilots learned that flying in coordinated groups offered them better protection and greater offensive capability, reducing their losses and increasing their victories. In the absence of radios, they communicated with hand signals or movements of the plane, such as a wag of the rudder or the rocking of wings. Recognizing one another was easy: the Allies tied streamers to the struts of their aircraft, while their enemies flew planes painted in loud, heraldic patterns.

In the Second World War, the British favoured the three-ship, V-shaped Vic formation that looked impressive in parade flypasts but had few, if any, tactical advantages. The Americans opted for the four-ship diamond formation and placed the least experienced pilot at the back, which did little for his already limited life expectancy. But during the Spanish Civil War, the German Condor Legion had developed the finger-four, so-called because, when viewed from above, it resembled the four fingertips of the right hand. By the end of the Second World War, nearly all air forces were using the finger-four.

The Cessna and the Smith employed the basic two-ship element of leader and wingman. The Cessna seemed big and ungainly, but she was the faster aircraft. Bojan had throttled back to slow cruise so that the Smith could cling to the Cessna's wing without straining her own engine. Because my eyes were fixed solidly upon my leader, I wasn't immediately aware of our speed as we hurtled across the countryside. That's why the lead pilot must execute any changes predictably and smoothly. If, at any time, the flying lulls them into thinking they are alone, the results could be catastrophic.

I settled into enjoying the close-quarters work. It was invigorating, just like when I first started learning aerobatics. After an hour, the Cessna waggled her wings and broke away to the south for home. I raised my gloved hand in farewell and made a slight course correction to the right for Rockcliffe. We'd already promised to meet later to debrief the flight, perhaps over lunch or a second cup of coffee. I watched the Cessna fade away, silently wished them a happy return, and turned my attention to my own.

Waving goodbye to my mates as they head home and I return to Rockcliffe Airport. (Photograph courtesy of Ernie Szelepcsenyi)

A couple of months later, I flew formation again, this time as leader. My wingman is Chris Ricci, flying a pudgy little Aeronca Champ. I'd known Chris since he joined Rockcliffe in 2015, replacing Simon Garrett as the chief flying instructor. Chris drew his energy from the inherent promise of the job. Like me, he was relatively young, but he had much of the old school in him. He had an affinity for the beauty and simplicity of taildraggers, aerobatics, and formation flying.

The Champ showed up at Rockcliffe in the same year as Chris. She was a fine example of the '46 vintage: white with two-tone blue trim, fat tires, and shiny chrome hubcaps. Like the Smith, she was the only one of her kind at Rockcliffe. Most pilots who learned to fly between the end of the Second World War and the early seventies trained in a Champ; my dad flew one at Collingwood when he was preparing for his own Smith. The mere sight of the little taildragger evokes the excitement of that first solo flight. If you ask an old hand, they'll tell you the Champ is a charming plane that can just barely kill you. It's true Champs are not particularly fast and don't do any one thing particularly well, but they're forgiving and docile, and are simply a lot of fun to fly. It didn't take Chris long to seek out the Champ's owners and work out an arrangement: flight instruction in exchange for use of their plane, plus gas.

On Chris's list of goals was an aerobatic instructor rating. As the club's only aerobatic instructor pilot, it fell to me to help get him there. Whenever time and money allowed, we shoehorned ourselves into the Super Decathlon and began building on his existing experience in aerobatics. Aviation, and in particular an aerobatic airplane, is a crucible in which friendships are born or die. One needs little time to discover which it will be. With Chris, it was clear that we would get along.

The Smith and Champ are well paired for formation flying. The July evening was shockingly cool and breezy. Chris and I sat under the cover of the canvas hangar and planned our trip. Above, an ugly grey blanket of stratocumulus slid by at a decent clip. Just outside, the windsock strained against its metal bracket.

About fifteen minutes later, the Smith and I climbed out of Rockcliffe and turned left to follow the Ottawa River west. As soon as we levelled out at circuit height, I throttled back to allow the Champ, which climbs at a speed barely faster than the one at which the Smith stalls, to catch up.

It took Chris a few miles, but by the time we rounded the southern end of the Gatineau Hills and headed northwest, the Champ slid into position off the Smith's right wings. I glanced over to make sure all was well. Chris gave me a curt nod. Eyes front again, I busied myself with the duties of a flight leader.

In short order, I discovered that the Smith's ninety miles per hour translated into about eighty-five for Chris and the Champ — a good formation flying speed. We climbed to two thousand feet in the hope that the ride would be smoother higher up. It wasn't, and every so often the wind slammed against our formation. On the wing, Chris and the Champ clung on grimly, bouncing up and down in the current.

The sky was grey and the land below was sallow. The Ottawa River, now off to our left and meandering north toward a sharp turn at Pontiac, was of similar complexion save for a few shimmering bands where the evening sunlight broke through the clouds.

I did a quick scan of the instrumentation: speed ninety, altitude 2,050, engine gauges green. A glance at the drunken compass provoked a chuckle before I focussed again on watching for other traffic.

"Lead, two." Chris's voice crackled in my ears. We limited our voice communication because the Champ didn't have an alternator and the radio drew from the battery. "Going echelon left."

"Lead," I acknowledged.

I glanced over as the Champ backed away slowly and then sank out of sight below my tail. Not having eyes on the Champ was unnerving, but I relied on trust and focussed on keeping my flying as precise and steady as my abilities allowed. Moments later, the Champ resurfaced on the left wings. Another nod from Chris.

We pushed on as far as Luskville before angling toward the escarpment to open up a wide turn to the left. Chris masterfully kept station on the inside wing as I guided us back toward Rockcliffe. Formation flying truly is great fun. I couldn't help but think of Charlie Miller and Gordon Skerratt. I reflect that, had my dad not purchased *Foxtrot*

Alpha Mike from Charlie nearly thirty years earlier, my flight with
Chris and everything it represented simply wouldn't be.

It was about a quarter to nine by the time our two-ship formation
was over Rockcliffe.

"Low pass?" Chris asked.

"Good idea," I responded.

We began a wide and gradual descending spiral to shed altitude.
The wind had died off, so the abrupt jolts were fewer and further
between. Chris kept station as we rounded out onto final approach and
swept across the field in formation. My radio calls and the combined
noise of our engines attracted a small group to the runway's edge to
witness our low pass across the airport.

As the end of the field approached, I went to full throttle and peeled
away to the north. Chris maintained runway heading to allow me the
space and time to rejoin the circuit, land, and taxi clear.

A few minutes later I used the light of the radio to jot down notes.
Over the swish of the prop, I heard Chris call, "Turning short final,"
and glanced up to see the Champ's silhouette glide in over the western
fence. It appeared to stop abruptly in mid-air and hover only inches
above the runway before dropping onto all three wheels. The wings
rocked slightly as the little plane slowed.

Chris taxied off and sidled up next to the Smith. I raised my hand
in greeting. He and the Champ appeared only as a silhouette, backlit
by the last light of a dying day, but I could tell he was smiling at the
promise of a new tradition.

☻

Aviation is heavy with rituals, and the walk-around inspection carries
perhaps the most weight of them all. It can be slow and thorough or
quick and cursory, depending on the pilot's sense of self-preservation.
But an $80-million airliner once crashed because workers had cov-
ered the exterior instruments with masking tape before washing down
the plane and then forgot to remove the tape. The tape blocked the

instruments and prevented the crew from reading their airspeed and altitude accurately. I favour slow and thorough.

I know the Smith well, and yet a walk-around inspection takes me about ten minutes, more if I need to replenish oil, lubricate a part, or adjust a loose inspection plate.

I'd already checked the weather: light winds and clear skies, save for the scattering of cumulus floating overhead. A few minutes later, I climbed over the cockpit rim and lowered myself into the fibreglass seat. I strapped in, took my gloves off the narrow glare shield, slipped them on, and reached out to pick my helmet up off of the cowling and place it in my lap.

I scribbled in my notebook as the next ritual begins: start up.

Throttle — set half to one inch open.

Carb heat — off.

Prime — three strokes.

Magnetos — both.

Stick — full aft.

Starter — engage.

I heard the battery relay click behind my head and the starter motor spin, but the propeller struggled to turn. I'd noticed the starter beginning to fail in recent weeks. Another blip of the starter, the propeller swung around — once, twice — and the Lycoming engine coughed to life.

The engine settled into a steady hum of a thousand revolutions per minute. As the Lycoming engineers have prescribed, I waited until the engine reached at least two hundred degrees at the cylinder heads before advancing the throttle beyond 1,200 rpm. Next, I checked the engine to confirm it could produce power under various settings. This check is no guarantee against failure during flight. Rather, it is a final opportunity to uncover any mechanical problems before casting off into the sky, where the options are limited and the results often tragic.

Satisfied that all was well, we took to the sky. I rolled my shoulders back and allowed my spine to fall against the seat. My right hand's grip on the stick relaxed as my left hand flexed around the throttle, shedding any residual tension. A flick of the wrist produced an instant response from the wings. Sounds faded, melting into a whisper of engine, wind, wires, and heart.

We floated across Gatineau and along the hills to Pontiac then across the river to Buckham's Bay. We doubled back north, overflew Mohr Island, and retraced our route in reverse. I've spent the majority of my flying life above these hills, fields, lakes, and rivers, and I always manage to spy something new, interesting, and inspiring.

Suddenly, the radio crackled to life. The Champ, with Chris at the controls, was rounding the southern tip of the escarpment and entering the practice area.

"*Lima Lima, Sierra Alpha*," I called out.

"Hey," answered Chris. "Formation?"

"Why not?"

We quickly reviewed the parameters. We'd rendezvous over Breckenridge at two thousand feet, and the Smith would fly lead. I set up a wide orbit over the town so that Chris, climbing slowly toward us, could visually make contact and form up.

The Champ does not fly quickly and climbs even slower. Given my higher altitude, it was more likely that he'd see me first. All the same, I pushed my goggles up and scanned the countryside below. After a short while, I picked out a tiny smudge of white emerging from the green of the escarpment. Before long, the smudge sprouted wings and a tail.

"I've got you," Chris reported over the radio. "My ten o'clock by about two miles."

It was the opportunity I'd been waiting for, and that morning, I couldn't help myself. I rocked my wings and called over the radio, "Tally-ho!"

The Champ continued to climb, hanging on the whirling disc of the prop. She hardly seemed to be moving. I watched as Chris checked the climb and turned toward us before accelerating and sliding into echelon left.

*The Champ (right) leads the Smith across the field at Rockcliffe,
summer of 2016.* (Photograph courtesy of Ernie Szelepcsenyi)

"Two on station," crackled his voice.

"Lead," I acknowledged.

For the next twenty minutes, our formation plied back and forth
between Breckenridge and Luskville. We practised turns as well as
climbs and descents. I concentrated on giving Chris the most stable of
platforms to fly off, and he did a nice job holding position. I led us in
a descent to the southeast and then around the tip of the escarpment
to overfly Gatineau. Abeam the Chelsea Dam, we climbed to seventeen
hundred feet and prepared for an overhead arrival at Rockcliffe for
another formation low pass. Throughout, the Smith and the Champ
flew as one.

It had been a sleepy morning at Rockcliffe. Our arrival and the
combined roar of our engines shattered the peace.

Rockcliffe's face has changed over the years. One runway has been
erased completely. Another now serves as the taxiway. Her expansive

military hangars are gone, leaving only the faint footprint of their foundations and the occasional iron tie-down ring. The unmistakeable song of the Merlin engine and the bass rumble of the old radials have long since faded, replaced by a chorus of small Lycomings and Continentals with the occasional refrain of a Kinner and Jacobs thrown in. Some purists might regard these changes as the equivalent of tearing down a national monument, but most of us are just glad the old field still exists.

It is the last undeveloped land in Canada's capital, and its once substantial footprint is dwindling. Years ago, the airport was bordered to the south by homes for the men and women stationed there, as well as a school, theatre, recreation centre, baseball diamonds, and a general store. Now heavy construction equipment shuttles back and forth just outside the airport's boundary, digging a drainage system for the new development on the stony bluffs from which the airfield takes its name. The presence of the Canada Aviation and Space Museum should secure Rockcliffe's future, but talk of an interprovincial bridge threatened the airfield in the 2000s. Once the neighbours in the new development realize an airport's actual purpose, it will likely come under scrutiny again.

Everyone who comes here leaves a piece of themselves behind. The flat patch of land has absorbed a century's worth of echoes. They give the airport her soul.

Rockcliffe is a grand old lady, and as Chris and I pass, I can't help but wonder if she finds us amusing. After all, the Lancaster's Merlins and Flying Fortress's Wright Cyclones once rattled her windowpanes. In those days, flypasts would stop conversations cold, if only because the participants could not hear each other well enough to continue. Now, only a few people stop to watch.

As we crossed the eastern perimeter fence and eased into a climb, I waved Chris off to join the crosswind for the circuit to land. The Smith and I continued climbing to the east and would join the circuit

(top) An aerial shot of the Rockcliffe Airbase in 1943 shows the triangular shape of the three runways as well as the various hangars and support buildings. (Photograph courtesy of Canada, Department of National Defence, Library and Archives Canada, PA-064459)

(above) The Rockcliffe Airport in September 2017.
(Photograph courtesy of Chuck Clark)

behind the Champ — mindful to give him a wider berth to allow for our faster approach speed.

In the shade of the hangar, another ritual: brakes on, throttle idle, magnetos to off then on again, one by one. I throttled up to 1,700 rpm and slowly drew out the red mixture control until the engine gave a final sigh and the propeller ticked slowly to a stop. Switches off, helmet off, gloves off.

To the ticking sound of the cooling engine, I unfolded myself from the cockpit and stretched out my back, running a hand along the biplane's long cowling. I rubbed my fingers together and retreated into the hangar to rummage through the Smith's kit box. I emerged again into the sunshine with a spray bottle and a blue shop cloth. The last ritual of the morning: wiping the smashed bugs off my little biplane.

Sixteen

Shortly after the fifth season with my Smith began, I passed a thousand hours aloft. When I first earned my wings, a thousand hours seemed unattainable. But it's a paltry sum, barely the equivalent of forty-two days in the sky; former classmates who fly for the military or commercial airlines have accumulated five times that amount. On this late summer evening, I share the flaming red sky with pilots who have ten, twenty, even thirty times the hours aloft. They've spent their adulthoods on wings. And, far above us all, are the select few who venture into the inhospitable expanse of space. I know my true insignificance.

And yet, we all secretly envy one another. The crew of the regional jet cruising just overhead, descending gently in the still air toward the capital's international airport, may wish their charge was a much larger craft, flying far above them in the opposite direction, bound for Paris, perhaps, or Milan. The crew of that international flight might find themselves thinking of their eventual retirement and a single-seat biplane in a quiet grass field. I, however, will almost certainly always occupy my current station. And I am content.

The radio crackles to life, and I wince. Somewhere between the small jet and me is another plane. The voice in my ears is hard, contemptuous, and officious. I know the type: an aspirant too proud to consider himself a lowly apprentice. He wields his voice as a swashbuckler brandishes his rapier, and yet the skill with which he handles his airplane betrays the newness of his wings.

He informs me that I've trespassed in his parcel of sky. He's practising spins and must have dominion from nearly four thousand feet all the way down to the earth below. I consider pointing out that, should he still find himself spinning when he reaches me, he'll most certainly have more pressing concerns. Instead, I promise to remain well clear.

On an evening such as this, I can't resist taking stock. I've led a charmed flying life. From common and humble beginnings in a two-seat trainer out of a small field on the St. Lawrence, I grew to fly airplanes most pilots only ever dream of: warbirds that carry forward the lessons of history; high-performance aerobatic machines that made my heart race; and, of course, my unique little biplane. I learned at the knee of good teachers, my dad included. At a relatively young age, I joined the small fraternity of aerobatic instructors. More than half of my flying career, if it can be called that, has been upside down. I've made my share of mistakes and survived to learn from them. Despite several opportunities, I've never put as much as a scratch on an airplane and, by some miracle, have dodged the misfortunes that often befall aviators before their logbook feels the weight of a thousand hours.

I've had five years of flying this wonderful little anachronism born of a California dreamer and held together with wires and faith. In some 150 hours aloft in this open-air, leather-trimmed cockpit, I have tasted fear, shouted with glee, felt my heart soar under the gentle push of these stubby wings, and beheld beauty scarcely seen by the earthbound: nascent moons and dying suns, rainbows cast against the tops of billowing clouds, rain falling earthward only to evaporate before reaching the ground. I know the personality of each instrument: the compass — a drunk; the vertical speed indicator — an optimist; and the airspeed indicator — a saint. I can manipulate every lever and knob in the tiny cockpit without looking, and I know not to ignore the mixture knob for too long lest its habit of creeping aft choke the engine. I know that the wires bracing the left wing tremble more than their counterparts to my right and could stand to be tightened. I've given a measure of myself to the biplane, and she has etched much of herself onto me. It feels like that first heart-thumping flight and near disastrous landing at Brampton happened a lifetime ago.

I feel safe up here despite the inherent dangers. In this cockpit, perhaps more than most, life is beautifully simple. It's measured in miles per hour, feet per minute, and gallons per hour. The mechanics of flying are so ridiculously easy that one wonders why more don't take it up. Then again, I can't help feeling jealously protective. I'm happy to admit guests to this sanctum but would prefer fewer permanent residents. The sky is a refuge for me. Life is easier to manage because I fly.

I don't like visiting my father's grave. I don't think it holds anything of him — or rather, anything of worth. It's why I feel closer to him in the air than I do on the ground. It's why I insisted on having his Smith engraved on the crypt's plaque. It's the reason for the airplane I'm sitting in, two thousand feet above the ground.

In ten years' time, when my biplane turns fifty and is showing her age, I might take her to a small grass strip carved out of a wide forest, to an aircraft fabric shop. They will strip away her fabric skin to expose the bones of steel and spruce beneath. With keen eyes and a careful touch, they will comb over her every inch and heal any ailments she may have picked up in her five decades aloft. Six months, or perhaps a year later, she will emerge into the light of a cool spring morning, refurbished and reborn. Ten or twenty years beyond that I might consider myself too old to handle this airplane with absolute certainty. At that point, might my son or daughter take up the torch and carry this story over the next horizon?

I ease the biplane into a turn. A glance down at the low wing reveals that the airplane is perfectly balanced on a wingtip, as the earth — deep browns, wet greens, and steely greys — whirls round below.

I lessen the bank angle, increase aft stick, and the Smith leaves the steady plane of the turn and bounds upward into a chandelle. Because of her high drag, the Smith bleeds energy like nothing else, and as we

finish the manoeuvre, she flops into level flight again and dips her
nose.

As the airspeed builds, a quiver passes through the airframe. The
wires buzz and whine — the sound building in intensity, hand in hand
with our velocity along this downward slope. The bellow of the slipstream now overpowers the engine's sonorous moan. Brisk aft stick
now, needing far more muscle than any aileron movement would.
The Smith lifts her nose, the horizon falls away, and we roll left as we
continue to climb. My left hand moves forward and the engine roars
in response. The horizon slides into view again, our wings cleaving it
neatly in two.

And then, life slows down, inching, crawling to a near stop. It's
quiet, although the engine is emphatically pushing out nearly full
power. The wires are still, glinting mischievously in the sun. I can hear
my heart thumping in my head. I've reached this apex many a time,
and with each visit, it feels like I'm here a little while longer.

The horizon slides up, and we're accelerating earthward again. I
slowly roll out, aiming for a green-roofed farmhouse and silo with a
red-and-white starburst dome. I imagine I am Willy Coppens, pressing home one of thirty-five successful attacks on barrage balloons, or
James McCudden, moments before shooting up a trench, or Werner
Voss, doubling back in attack against a hapless foe in the First World
War.

Of late, my father's ghost has grown fond of holding up a mirror.
Pre-flight inspections now take more time, and I linger longer in certain areas. The rituals — the very ones meant to assuage one's fears
that this flight might be your last — don't convince me as they once
did. Occasionally, but with increasing regularity, the reasons to fly are
overruled by the safety and security in remaining earthbound. For
the first time in my life, I feel a measure of guilt. Our daughter Evelyn
Anne was born on a mild mid-January day in 2017. Unlike her more
leisurely brother, she took less than an hour to storm onto the scene.
Why am I flying with the birds rather than reading stories to my kids,

and what will become of them if something happens to me during a flight? I think of my nineteen-year-old self and the bravado with which I made the definitive statement on my longevity as an aviator. I think of my dad and his cold feet. Now, I know the chill.

One day, you might understand…

My dad's words echo in my head. I can hear him plainly. His voice is gentle, almost apologetic as it was near the end, when the edge of bitterness and anger had worn away.

I took this self-portrait near Rockland, Ontario, November 2014, using a strut-mounted camera.

I've now three times his experience, both in this airplane and in total time aloft. Might I be blessed with five hundred hours more? A thousand? Or will this hour be my last? And what if I hang up my wings? I might be alive, yes, but I would hardly be living, and with no guarantee that some other calamity might not befall me.

It almost surprises me, how much I miss him. After all, he only really lived with us until I was about ten. I've spent more of my life without him. When he was away for work, we spoke on the phone almost every day, but nothing can replace in-the-flesh contact,

(top) My mom and me with Foxtrot Alpha Mike *at Rockcliffe Airport, in June 1984. This is my only photograph with the airplane. (bottom) We recreated the photograph with my wife and son in the fall of 2015.*

support, and guidance whenever you need it. My father missed the critical years, when my character was truly formed. When I was about fifteen years old, I told Mom that I didn't know what kind of father I would be, but I knew very well what sort I *wouldn't* be. It was a biting and clear shot at my father.

And yet, whether through nature or nurture, I absorbed many of the qualities I think are essential for being a good father from him. I'm blessed with his patience, which was nearly boundless, at least for me and my sister. He would always try to reason with us, as though we were much older and more mature than we were, and I find myself doing the same with my own son, even though he's probably not old enough to really understand. It's a legacy from the past: my dad learned it from his father, and I see it as laying the groundwork for the future.

When Elgin was two and a half, I sat him on my lap, strapped my harness around us both, and taxied him around Rockcliffe in my Smith. Evelyn, not quite six months old, glared at us from her stroller. An hour later, they watched as I climbed into a Second World War trainer, a Fairchild Cornell built two years before their grandfather was born, for a short air display before I returned it to its home base a short flight away.

Elgin and Evelyn with DSA *at Rockcliffe Airport in the summer of 2018.*

Watching the airliners take off and land at the international airport near our home quickly became an after-dinner summer pastime for the kids. They love the novelty of sitting on the roof of the family car and competing to be the first to spot the landing lights of an incoming airliner as it turns onto the final approach. Elgin knows why a turbo-prop sounds different than a jet and thinks jet exhaust smells like barbecue. He enjoys pointing out airplanes during car rides and while Evelyn's vocabulary isn't as extensive as his, you can tell she's excited to see something flying through the sky. Sometimes, I'm the one flying above them. One summer, as the kids frolicked in a backyard pool belonging to family friends, I took the Smith out and orbited overhead, waggling my wings in greeting. In a few years, I'll happily take them for a flight in the Decathlon or one of the Cessnas rented from the club, something I had to wait a long time to do with my own father. When they're old enough, and if they're interested, I might finish my regular flight instructor rating, find a little Champ taildragger, and teach them to fly.

I've come to realize that my dad died twice. The father of my birth — easy-going, confident, youthful, almost happy-go-lucky — faded away when his company failed and he folded his wings. In his place stood a man who was preoccupied, obsessed, and mercurial at times. He was still a loving father and gave the impression of handling things, but in truth he was stuck in a loop of self-doubt and despair. I resented him at times, but I loved him. And I know he loved me.

Today's time has passed. Soon, there will not be enough light to navigate. We turn for home. The sun lies low on the western horizon. The sky above is nearly white. I squint against the brightness, cursing myself for not wearing the prescription sunglasses I've only just purchased for this exact situation.

A dark shadow passes in front of my eyes. It's so sudden that I nearly slam the stick to the right to avoid a mid-air collision with another airplane I've failed to see in the sun's glare. Instead, I draw a steadying breath and take no action. We are still flying and the shadow remains stationary, hanging in the hot disc of the sun. It's a familiar silhouette: a little biplane with wings laid one upon the other, and joined by struts and wires. The whirl of the propeller glows. I bank my wings gently to the left. A fraction of a second later, the biplane matches our movements exactly.

At first, I think we are chasing our own shadow. But it can't be so. The sun is ahead and not behind. Our accidental quarry is most certainly another airplane. The shape of the tail is different, for one, and this ship has fairings around the wheels that resemble the extended talons of a bird of prey.

As we creep closer, I can make out wings and tail of cherry red slashed with white, the same red across the fuselage but cleaved with a wide white band from cockpit to tail where, with some squinting, I can read the registration letters.

C-FFAM.

It cannot be, and yet it is.

I slot my Smith in on the lead Smith's right wing, perhaps fifteen feet distant. The white-helmeted pilot nods and slightly rocks his wings.

We plow onward, roughly west by northwest. Aloft, we slide along this invisible current with nary a ripple.

I once asked my dad what he might like to do when he retired.

"Retire?" he repeated, incredulously. "I won't retire."

"Okay, well, what if you had, say, two months to do whatever you wanted to?"

"Well..." He paused and thought a while before smiling. "We'd get two airplanes and fly across the country."

His Smith has drifted in front of the sun, a violent magenta now, as it begins to dip below the distant horizon. The air around *FAM*'s exhaust pipes shimmers and roils. The wings, fabric taut over fifty-year-old spruce ribs, glow. Here, framed between the wings and wires of my biplane, is an image that is for me alone. Dad's Smith dips her

The flight that never was. (Painting by Laura Psutka)

left wings and starts a slight turn toward the clear patch of land that is our home and destination. We follow.

As we roll out, the last light of this September evening spills over our wings and dances across my instrument panel. Below, the valley is still, quiet, and dark. Beyond, on the distant horizon, the lights of the city wink on, seemingly one by one, to guide us home.

As we sweep over the airport, *Foxtrot Alpha Mike* banks sharply to the right and breaks away to land. I continue north as I watch the little biplane arc away and down — my dad's preferred gliding approach, a 180-degree turn finishing just above the numbers that identify Rockcliffe's remaining runway. Red-and-white starburst against the deep green of the land, he sweeps over the trees to the east of the field, across the perimeter road and then the boundary fence. As he descends and slows, *FAM*'s brilliant colour fades, as though its existence in this world depends on altitude and speed. The Smith reaches the runway and is committed to land. She's barely visible as her nose rises gently so that the landing gear meets the asphalt at the proper angle. And then, they're gone.

My Smith and I land at Rockcliffe just before night falls, taxi past the small plot of land where *Foxtrot Alpha Mike* once lived, and shut down just outside our little hangar. In the light of the sun's last gasp, I run a damp rag across the Smith's cowling and the leading edges of each wing. Not a bug. Not a single one. It is as though we never left the ground at all.

I can hear the soft ticking of the cylinders cooling. My hand can feel the warmth of a tired engine beneath the cowling. Even the gas gauge, as fallible as it may be, indicates we burned some five gallons of fuel. While parts of this flight were fantasy, others were rooted firmly in reality. Somehow, we found a current aloft that bridged the two worlds so that we could fly together once more.

Epilogue

On a warm summer day, my wife, the kids, and I make the three-hour drive to the Granby Zoo. Ostensibly, we're making the trip because our son loves animals and has only seen elephants, zebras, and giraffes in books. But I, of course, want to see where my dad's biplane has ended up. It's been more than five years since Dad died, and I finally feel ready.

Elgin has ignored our suggestions that he nap and stayed awake — and kept his baby sister awake — for the entire drive. In his lap is a pile of jungle animal magnets. He's gone through each one several times, holding it up and asking if we will see its real-life counterpart at the zoo.

The Smith is in the Africa exhibit, which seems fitting, given my father learned to fly in Eastern Africa. We view elephants, zebra, giraffes, ostriches, and marabou. As the elephant ambles toward us, I hoist my son onto my shoulders so he can have a better look.

We leave the elephants behind and round a bend on our way to the flamingos. Jutting out from behind a cluster of trees is the unmistakeable shape of a Smith biplane's tail. This is the closest I've been to my dad's plane in thirty years. For a moment, I consider abandoning my family and cutting across the walkway and the lawn of tall grass beyond to lay a hand on her cowls. But my son has other ideas, and he leads me along the path toward the flamingos.

The flamingos high-step through a small pond choked with lily pads. We move on to the lion's den and a glass enclosure housing a formidable gorilla. My son seems interested at first but cowers behind my legs when the gorilla comes close. Next, we visit with a giant tortoise and a pack of ring-tailed lemurs before rounding another bend and emerging into a clearing. And there she is.

The airplane is covered in fibreglass and a coat of bright orange paint with slashes of blue and white. She's unmistakeably a Smith: straight wings, N-struts, long cowl narrowing toward the cockpit. The landing gear is crumpled up beneath the lower wing, splayed out as though her arrival in this strange place was violent and sudden. The fuel cap and the propeller hub remain, but the propeller is gone. The radio antenna housing is still in place, but the antenna has been removed. About two feet of the upper wing, nearest the right tip, is missing, and so are the stainless steel wires that once braced the wings. Someone unfamiliar with airplanes has put her back together. The lower wings have been turned over and reversed so that the aileron hinges are visible. A piece of plywood has been placed in the cockpit so that kids can get in and out with ease. I wonder if the Smith's unique control column, the one Larry Butt recognized in Orillia all those years ago, is under the makeshift plywood seat.

To the casual eye, it would appear some intrepid pilot crashed in the African desert dunes, perhaps on a mail run or, as was the fashion in the early days of aviation, a record-breaking flight. Perhaps he committed the fatal error of leaving his machine in search of salvation, only to be swallowed by the sand. The scene evokes shades of Antoine de Saint-Exupéry's *The Little Prince*, and I suspect that's rather the point.

My boy, a little younger than the Little Prince, regards the plane with suspicion, perhaps wondering how it came to be in the zoo. A half-dozen children clamber over it: two wedged in the cockpit, one riding astride the nose, another hopping up and down on the top wing. As the boy on the top wing jumps with a thud onto the lower wing, I remind myself that she is no longer an airplane but a children's plaything.

My son with his grandfather's biplane in her new,
hopefully permanent role.

"Loop, Da-da," my son says, pointing (at the time he pronounced *k* as *p*). "A biplane!"

"Nonno's biplane," I reply, using the Italian word for grandfather.

"Nonno's biplane…" he repeats with a degree of uncertainty. He's seen the picture on the fireplace mantle at home, the one of the grandfather he'll never meet. My dad is in jeans and a blue T-shirt, frozen in mid-stride as he walks past the biplane's nose, white helmet hanging from one hand. This biplane doesn't look much like the one in the picture.

I hoist my son into the cockpit. I wonder how my dad would feel if he could see this, his first grandchild sitting in the cockpit of the airplane he treasured.

As we walk away, I take a final look back, remembering when I was four and last took in this view. For me and my children, she is a lasting monument to my dad and his undying love of flight. I am sad that she will never fly again, but I am overjoyed to know that, in the hearts and minds of the children who climb into her single seat, she takes flight, every day.

Acknowledgements

I'll start by thanking you, the reader, for picking up the book in the first place and getting this far. I hope you saw something of yourself in the book and that it did, in some part, inspire you to chase down your own dreams. Please believe me when I tell you that it's worth it, no matter how difficult it might be.

Thank you to publisher Susanne Alexander, acquisitions editor Karen Pinchin, production editor Alan Sheppard, creative director Julie Scriver, copy editor Kathryn Hayward, and the entire team at Goose Lane Editions for your belief in me and in the story, your guidance throughout, and ultimately your care of the book.

I didn't write an essay until my last year of high school English. I had two influential teachers, Stephen Durnin and Muriel McQuillan. They stoked my love of writing rather than smothering it under a mountain of academic papers — encouraging me to write poetry, short stories, plays, and, one time, an alternate ending to *A Tale of Two Cities*. I remain eternally grateful to both of you.

I'd like to acknowledge my friend and former colleague Norman Fetterley, who set all of this in motion by encouraging me to seek out a publisher. Likewise, this book would not be what it is without Edward Soye, Al Girdvainis, and Patrick Giunta who were instrumental in my acquisition of *Delta Sierra Alpha*.

While this is not a scholarly work, it did require a fair amount of research. I am indebted to Murray Sinton, Lee Heitman, Larry Butt, Ernie Muller, Michel Lequin, Alain Maille, and especially Charlie Miller, for their generous help in tracing my father's flying life and *Foxtrot Alpha Mike*'s history. Much of the colour in the early part of the book is due to Charlie opening up his records, stories, and memories to me. I hope I've done well by you, Charlie.

I am forever grateful to my editor, Jill Ainsley, for helping me to draw out and feature the heart and soul of the story. Writing a book is a difficult endeavour, particularly if you're doing it for the first time, and having Jill to both champion and challenge me was invaluable. Thank you, Jill. *Airborne* is a better book because of you.

And finally, my heartfelt thanks to my family, particularly my dad, mom, sister, wife, and children for their unwavering support throughout this journey and in all aspects of my life, always. I love you.

Jonathan Rotondo is a writer, recovering journalist, and biplane pilot who spent his childhood hanging off airport perimeter fences throughout Ontario and Quebec, where his passion for flight first took hold.

He has worked as a journalist and television producer and in military public affairs and media relations. A long-time aviator, Jonathan spends his free time teaching other pilots aerobatic maneuvers, retracing his father's flying in his 1978 Smith Miniplane, and writing about aviation for the Canadian Owners and Pilots Association and *Canadian Aviator* magazine. He lives in Ottawa.

Photo: Robert Patterson